DELIGHTING
IN THE LORD
THROUGH THE PSALMS

BRIAN GREUTMAN

Tom & Patti –
Blessings to you
delight in Him

Delighting in the Lord Through the Psalms
Copyright 2015 Brian M. Greutman
All rights reserved

Greutman, Brian, 1973-, author
Delighting in the Lord: through the Psalms/Brian Greutman
ISBN 978-0-692-51466-5

Design by Todd Schlosser / www.ledstudios.com
Printed by Diggy POD, Tecumseh, Michigan

Table of Contents

Acknowledgements

This entire project wouldn't be possible without the help of many people. Thanks to my wonderful wife Gretchen for your support and help on the home front as I worked on this project. I am so blessed to have you by my side. It is a joy to share life with you. I love you! Nathan, Nicholas, and Noah, thanks for your enthusiasm, love, and patience.

Thanks to Pastor Andy Rosas and Riverview Community Church for the gift of a sabbatical from ministry in 2014 as it inspired this devotional project. It has been a pleasure serving the people of Riverview for the last twelve years and I look forward to the future!

Thank you to Todd Schlosser for doing the artwork, layout, and design, for this book. Thanks for believing in the heart behind and vision for this project. You are a huge blessing!

I'm so grateful for the following people who helped edit this book: Pastor Dennis Sawyer, Pastor Brett Hollis, Dr. Steve Brown, and John Van Lierop Jr. I appreciate the time and effort you spent to help me communicate in the best way possible! Thanks to my men's group for going through the devotional with me: Randy Davis, Jacob Popoff, David Owens, John Machowski, and Todd Schlosser. I appreciate your input. I'm grateful to Jeff Hoffman for doing the initial layout of the book. Thanks for believing in the project from the start.

Thanks to Sue Hoffman for all the great advice along the way.

Thanks to my parents Marrell and Terry Greutman for always believing in me and encouraging me to pursue the Lord and the dreams he lays on my heart. Thanks to my sister Heidi-Lyn and brother-in-law Dan Mensonides for your encouragement.

It has been a pleasure working with the Riverview Community Church staff over the years. Thanks to Pastor Andy Rosas, Ron Lalime, Sarah Tuttle, and Abel Foto for your friendship and partnership in ministry. The Riverview Worship Team has been a blessing to lead and serve alongside for twelve years. Your dedication to the Lord and worshiping him inspires me!

Thanks to my prayer partners Russell Booth and Jeff Fiorito for all the wonderful prayer times and for your ongoing support.

I am eternally grateful for the ministry of Arrow Leadership that has supported, encouraged, and challenged me in my leadership and ministry. Thanks to Dr. Steve Brown, Gretchen Englund, Pastor Scott Anderson, and Pastor Tim McCarthy in particular.

Preface

In the summer of 2014 I was given the gift of a sabbatical from my ministry as a pastor. At the beginning of that time I had allowed the pressures of life to drain me of my passion. As I began to write these devotionals from the Psalms seeking to delight in the Lord and his Word my passion for God, my family, and my ministry was renewed.

These devotionals are divided into seven weeks with one entry per day for a total of forty-nine entries. I have added one bonus devotional to make fifty. Each day includes a Psalm reading, devotional, two reflection questions, and a prayer. The accompanying piano CD has fifty corresponding compositions with titles that match the devotionals. The track number is given at the start of each devotional. You can listen to each song in the background as you read the corresponding devotional or listen to the CD on its own. (Which I hope you do!)

My prayer and hope is that you would be renewed in your passion for God as you read these Psalms and devotionals seeking to delight in the Lord and his Word. May the Lord fill you with his joy, strength, and encouragement as you seek to delight in him!

WEEK

1

DAY 1   Disc 1 / Track 1

Delighting in the Lord

Blessed is the one who does not walk in step with the wicked or stand in the way that sinners take or sit in the company of mockers, but whose delight is in the law of the LORD, and who meditates on his law day and night. That person is like a tree planted by streams of water, which yields its fruit in season and whose leaf does not wither—whatever they do prospers. Not so the wicked! They are like chaff that the wind blows away. Therefore the wicked will not stand in the judgment, nor sinners in the assembly of the righteous. For the Lord watches over the way of the righteous, but the way of the wicked leads to destruction.

PSALM 1:1-6

What do you want most in life? Most people would say that they want to be happy and successful. That of course can mean different things to different people. In this Psalm, David tells us the key to true happiness in life. It is in delighting in the "law of the LORD" and meditating on it all the time. We often think of laws as being restrictive and yet the "law of the LORD" brings true freedom in life.

Sometimes I obsess about things. A mental tape starts playing in my head and it's hard to stop. I've done this many times with a classical piano piece. This is similar to meditating on something. The dictionary definition of "meditate" is "to focus one's thoughts on (or to) reflect on or ponder over".[1] When we meditate on something we focus exclusively on that thing or in this case the "law of the LORD". Meditating on and delighting in God's law is delighting in God himself, the amazing things he has done, and his plans for us. When we do that we are like a tree that grows, prospers, and is fruitful.

However, those who follow the counsel of the wicked and their sinful ways are like chaff or the useless parts that the wind blows away. The wicked and their sinful ways will not last and will be judged. The promise for those who delight in the Lord is that God watches over us and he directs our steps. Psalm 37:23 says, "The steps of a good man are ordered by the LORD, And He delights in his way." (NKJV) If we are delighting in and valuing God and his law above all else then we can be assured that the Lord is delighting in us. What a promise!

What are you delighting in today? What do you look forward to in your day? Are you experiencing the assurance and peace that comes from knowing that God is watching over you today?

Delighting in the Lord can start by simply looking outside in the morning and thanking God for his beautiful creation and acknowledging that he is giving us another day to enjoy. Delighting in the Lord can be expressed in gratitude to him for the gift of our families and the people in our lives. Delighting in the Lord is seeking to please him in our workplace. Delighting in the Lord is seeking to give him glory in all we do. Colossians 3:17 says, "And whatever you do, whether in word or deed, do it all in the name of the Lord Jesus, giving thanks to God the Father through him." Let's strive to delight in God's law today knowing that doing so will make us truly happy and successful in life.

Reflection Questions

1. What brings you the most delight or joy in life?
2. What would help you delight in the Lord and his Word more?

Father, help me to delight in you and your law today. I want to please you in everything I do. Make me like a tree that grows and is fruitful daily.

DAY 2 Disc 1 / Track 2

Under Attack

LORD, how many are my foes! How many rise up against me! Many are saying of me, "God will not deliver him." But you, LORD, are a shield around me, my glory, the One who lifts my head high. I call out to the LORD, and he answers me from his holy mountain. I lie down and sleep; I wake again, because the LORD sustains me. I will not fear though tens of thousands assail me on every side. Arise, LORD! Deliver me, my God! Strike all my enemies on the jaw; break the teeth of the wicked. From the LORD comes deliverance. May your blessing be on your people.

PSALM 3:1-8

There are times in life when we feel surrounded by enemies. Sometimes these enemies are external and other times they are internal. People can accuse, attack, and threaten to ruin parts of our lives. Internal struggles with depression, anxiety, fear, anger, and the like can cause great trouble for us as well. King David writes this Psalm when he is fleeing because his son Absalom is threatening to take his kingdom away from him. He writes that God is his protector, encourager, and sustainer in those moments. David knows where true deliverance and help come from. Where do we turn when our enemies surround us?

There was a time in my life when I was overcome with anxiety and obsessive thoughts. However, through the wonderful ministry of Arrow Leadership[2], a Christian counselor, and those close to me, God brought me a pathway to deliverance. Through this experience I realized that God uses multiple means to achieve his purposes in our lives. I learned new ways to deal with these challenges from the counselor and I gained support from those close to me. I know that God led me to seek help from those sources. If I had only prayed and not talked with anyone I don't think things would have changed. In David's case I believe there were lessons he learned while on the run. In time his kingdom was restored with him securely on the throne.

Although God is concerned with our well-being and deliverance he is more concerned with his glory and his plans being accomplished in our lives. David understood this. Psalm 63:2-3 says, "I have seen you in the sanctuary and beheld your power and your glory. Because your love is better than life, my lips will glorify you." The Lord knows that when we are more concerned with his glory than anything else then we can experience his love as better than life. "You make known to me the path of life; you will fill me with joy in your presence, with eternal pleasures at your right hand" (Psalm 16:11). The joy of living for God and his glory is our strength when we are surrounded by our enemies and seeking deliverance and when we are in the best of times. God can be our joy at all times.

Reflection Questions

1. Think about a time you were under attack. What did you do?
2. How can focusing on God's glory and love help you when you're attacked?

Lord, help me to turn to you when I am under attack. I know that you love me and you are greater than my problems. Help me to live for you and your glory so that my strength and joy will be in you.

DAY 3 Disc 1 / Track 3

Created to Worship

LORD, our Lord, how majestic is your name in all the earth! You have set your glory in the heavens. Through the praise of children and infants you have established a stronghold against your enemies, to silence the foe and the avenger. When I consider your heavens, the work of your fingers, the moon and the stars, which you have set in place, what is mankind that you are mindful of them, human beings that you care for them? You have made them a little lower than the angels and crowned them with glory and honor. You made them rulers over the works of your hands; you put everything under their feet: all flocks and herds, and the animals of the wild, the birds in the sky, and the fish in the sea, all that swim the paths of the seas. LORD, our Lord, how majestic is your name in all the earth!

PSALM 8:1-9

It is not hard to see that humans were created to worship. God put in each of our hearts a desire to worship something greater than us. David begins this Psalm by saying how amazing God's name and is his glory are. Then he says that from the time we were infants God designed us to worship him. It's part of our DNA.

Then the Psalmist describes how the heavens, moon, and stars tell of God's glory as the Creator. He goes onto say how amazing it is that God cares for us. In fact, God has given mankind authority over creation to rule over it. He has put the animals in our control.

Many today are running to what Louie Giglio describes as "empty wells and puny gods" and are worshiping them.[3] People today worship Hollywood stars, musicians, money, and other things. However, we have the privilege of worshipping the God who created the world and who takes time for us. Jesus said in Matthew 6:26-27,

"Look at the birds of the air; they do not sow or reap or store away in barns, and yet your heavenly Father feeds them. Are you not much more valuable than they? Can any one of you by worrying add a single hour to your life?" Rather than spending our time worrying we should be spending our time worshipping.

It's amazing how our outlook in life changes when we focus on the greatness of the Lord. We realize how small our problems and struggles really are.

Psalm 34:8 says, "Taste and see that the LORD is good; blessed is the one who takes refuge in him." John Piper's book *Desiring God* has influenced my thinking on this topic. When we taste an amazing dish of pasta, a juicy steak, a latte, or our food of choice we like it and are convinced it is good. In the same way when we learn about the Lord through his Word, prayer, and worship we "taste" of his goodness and are convinced that he is amazingly satisfying.[4] Piper says, *"God is most glorified in us when we are most satisfied in Him".*[5] However this doesn't happen without an investment of time and energy on our part. Yet, when we do, we are fulfilling God's call on our lives and doing what we were created to do-worship!

Reflection Questions

1. What habits in your life show that you were created to worship?
2. Think about a time when you tasted of God's goodness. (Psalm 34:8) How did it affect you?

Lord I know that I was created to worship you. Teach me to be satisfied in you as I learn to live for your glory. I choose to spend my time today worshipping you rather than worrying.

DAY 4 Disc 1 / Track 4

Is God Hiding?

How long, LORD? Will you forget me forever? How long will you hide your face from me? How long must I wrestle with my thoughts and day after day have sorrow in my heart? How long will my enemy triumph over me? Look on me and answer, LORD my God. Give light to my eyes, or I will sleep in death, and my enemy will say, "I have overcome him," and my foes will rejoice when I fall. But I trust in your unfailing love; my heart rejoices in your salvation. I will sing the LORD's praise, for he has been good to me.

PSALM 13:1-6

There are times in life when we feel like God has forgotten us and is hiding from us. When writing this Psalm, David was in one of those times as he was extremely discouraged and full of sorrow. He felt like his enemies were winning and like he was going to die. He keeps asking God, "How long?"

When I was traveling with a summer music group in college this was the Psalm our speaker spoke on almost every night for three months. There were times when we thought, "How long are we going to have to hear this same message every night?"

I will never forget how he explained the change in David in the fifth verse of the Psalm. Everything had been doom and gloom and then David says, "But I trust in your unfailing love; my heart rejoices in your salvation" (v. 5). The speaker said that David remembered God's faithfulness to him in the past and most importantly he remembered God's character. God loves his children and delights in delivering them.

There have been pivotal times in my life when I had to trust that because God had been faithful to me in the past that he would be faithful me in the future. Hebrews 13:8, "Jesus Christ is the same yesterday and today and forever."

John Piper, in his book *Future Grace* says that in our fight against anxiety, depression, and other things we must put our faith and trust in God's future grace for us. We must trust that God, because of Jesus' death on the cross, will give us the grace we need to deal with situations five minutes from now, an hour from now, etc. Because of that we can choose to trust God instead of giving in to things like worry, fear, and anger.[6]

At the end of this Psalm David begins to sing and rejoice in God's goodness to him.

Rather than being anxious or depressed today let's trust that God will provide what we need moment by moment. Let's choose to rejoice in that today!

Reflection Questions

1. Have you ever felt like God was hiding from you? Why did you feel that way?
2. How does remembering God's faithfulness to you in the past help you in your present circumstances and as you think about the future?

Father, I trust that because you have been faithful to me in the past that you will be faithful to me in the future. Rather than giving in to negative thoughts, emotions, and actions today I choose to trust in you.

DAY 5 ● Disc 1 / Track 5

Our Safety is our Joy

Keep me safe, my God, for in you I take refuge. I say to the Lord, "You are my Lord; apart from you I have no good thing." I say of the holy people who are in the land, "They are the noble ones in whom is all my delight." Those who run after other gods will suffer more and more. I will not pour out libations of blood to such gods or take up their names on my lips. LORD, you alone are my portion and my cup; you make my lot secure. The boundary lines have fallen for me in pleasant places; surely I have a delightful inheritance. I will praise the LORD, who counsels me; even at night my heart instructs me. I keep my eyes always on the LORD. With him at my right hand, I will not be shaken. Therefore my heart is glad and my tongue rejoices; my body also will rest secure, because you will not abandon me to the realm of the dead, nor will you let your faithful one see decay. You make known to me the path of life; you will fill me with joy in your presence, with eternal pleasures at your right hand.

PSALM 16:1-11

What should we do when we need protection and safety in this life? David cried out to God seeking refuge in him knowing that those who looked to other sources would be disappointed.

The Psalmist knew that God was allowing the present circumstances in his life and that God was his provider. When life gets tough where do we turn first? Do we look to our friends, family, a counselor, or entertainment? Many people choose escape when life gets tough or even to numb the pain.

David said, "I will praise the LORD, who counsels me; even at night my heart instructs me" (v. 7). David looked to God as his counselor, his focus, and his security. Too often we forget just who God is.

Randy Alcorn writes, "Most of us would love to spend the evening with a great author, musician, artist, or head of state. God is the master artist who created the universe, the inventor of music, the author and main character of the unfolding drama of redemption."[7]

No wonder the final verse of the Psalm describes us being filled with joy in God's presence and eternal pleasures at his right hand. When we seek him for help or protection we can know that his joy is our strength now and in even greater ways in eternity when we are fully in his presence. Nehemiah 8:10 says, "...for the joy of the LORD is your strength." Are we allowing the "master artist" to fill us with joy by spending time in his presence daily? If so, we can confidently go forward in the strength he provides.

Reflection Questions

1. Where or to whom do you turn when life gets rough?
2. Does spending time with the Lord fill you with joy and strength, and confidence? Which spiritual disciplines (prayer, studying scripture, etc.) do that for you?

Lord give me a bigger picture of your greatness and power! I look to you for protection, counsel, and guidance. Fill me with your joy, strength, and confidence today because I have spent time with you.

DAY 6   Disc 1 / Track 6

Better Than Gold

The heavens declare the glory of God; the skies proclaim the work of his hands. Day after day they pour forth speech; night after night they reveal knowledge. They have no speech, they use no words; no sound is heard from them. Yet their voice goes out into all the earth, their words to the ends of the world. In the heavens God has pitched a tent for the sun. It is like a bridegroom coming out of his chamber, like a champion rejoicing to run his course. It rises at one end of the heavens and makes its circuit to the other; nothing is deprived of its warmth. The law of the Lord is perfect, refreshing the soul. The statutes of the Lord are trustworthy, making wise the simple. The precepts of the Lord are right, giving joy to the heart. The commands of the Lord are radiant, giving light to the eyes. The fear of the Lord is pure, enduring forever. The decrees of the Lord are firm, and all of them are righteous. They are more precious than gold, than much pure gold; they are sweeter than honey, than honey from the honeycomb. By them your servant is warned; in keeping them there is great reward. But who can discern their own errors? Forgive my hidden faults. Keep your servant also from willful sins; may they not rule over me. Then I will be blameless, innocent of great transgression. May these words of my mouth and this meditation of my heart be pleasing in your sight, Lord, my Rock and my Redeemer.

PSALM 19:1-14

I am writing this from Glacier, Washington, which is near Mt. Baker. When I look at the mountains, the nearby river, and the waterfalls, I see the glory of God. I cannot see the heavens but I can see the skies and they definitely proclaim the work of God's hands.

In this Psalm, David compares the sun to a bridegroom coming out of his tent or to a champion running his race. The sun faithfully gives us the provision we need.[8]

Then David begins to talk about the law of the Lord and what it does. It's almost as if David is saying that the law of the Lord is even more amazing than his creation.[9] God's law refreshes us, makes us wise, brings joy to our hearts, and gives light to our eyes. When we study God's Word we are changed. Our outlook on life changes and we begin to see the world the way he sees it.

David then says that God's ordinances or ways are better than pure gold and sweeter than honey from the honeycomb. David values God's law more than earthly riches and knows it's more desirable than the sweetest of foods. Do we value and desire God's law like that?

The Psalmist knows that the only way to avoid sin is by seeking to know and follow God's law. He ends by asking that his words and thoughts would be pleasing to the Lord. I have a pastor friend and mentor who prays this verse first thing every morning when he gets out of bed, "May these words of my mouth and this meditation of my heart be pleasing in your sight, LORD, my Rock and my Redeemer" (v. 14). What a great way to start our day!

Reflection Questions
1. Does creation inspire you to worship the Lord?
2. Do you value the Bible more than riches and great food? If not, what can you do to increase your passion for God's Word?

Father, I am amazed at your beautiful creation that you have given me to enjoy. Help me to be amazed at the perfection of your Word so that I will value it more than gold or riches, and the best of foods.

DAY 7 〜 ⬤ Disc 1 / Track 7

Proclaim His Name

I will declare your name to my people; in the assembly I will praise you. You who fear the LORD, praise him! All you descendants of Jacob, honor him! Revere him, all you descendants of Israel! For he has not despised or scorned the suffering of the afflicted one; he has not hidden his face from him but has listened to his cry for help. From you comes the theme of my praise in the great assembly; before those who fear you I will fulfill my vows. The poor will eat and be satisfied; those who seek the LORD will praise him—may your hearts live forever! All the ends of the earth will remember and turn to the LORD, and all the families of the nations will bow down before him, for dominion belongs to the LORD and he rules over the nations. All the rich of the earth will feast and worship; all who go down to the dust will kneel before him—those who cannot keep themselves alive. Posterity will serve him; future generations will be told about the LORD. They will proclaim his righteousness, declaring to a people yet unborn: He has done it!

PSALM 22:22-31

Psalm twenty-two begins with the Psalmist being far from God and feeling forsaken by God. Jesus quoted verse one when he was on the cross, "My God, my God, why have you forsaken me?" It goes on to explain the troubles and challenges of the Psalmist and then his deliverance from those. This Psalm was prophetic about Jesus on the cross but can be applied to our lives as well.[10]

Our reading picks up after the troubles have subsided in verse twenty-two. A different note of proclamation and praise is struck at this point. "I will declare your name to my people; in the assembly I will praise you" (v. 22). There is something powerful and special that happens when we worship God with other people. This can happen at church, a Bible study, a campfire, or in other places. There is also something exhilarating about declaring who God is corporately that is different from our personal time with God. In those moments we realize we are part of a larger group of followers and worshipers of God. We rejoice with those who are rejoicing and weep with those who are weeping (Romans 12:15).

This Psalm reminds us that God responds and helps those who are suffering and in trouble. "The LORD is close to the broken-hearted and saves those who are crushed in spirit" (Psalm 34:18). I remember praying for someone in a group setting who was going through a divorce at the time. Something welled up inside of me; tears of compassion started flowing out for this person. Perhaps I got just a glimpse of the love and compassion that Jesus has for us-especially in our times of need.

The end of this Psalm reminds us that people will worship the Lord from all over the earth. There will come a day when every knee will bow before him. "That at the name of Jesus every knee should bow, in heaven and on earth and under the earth" (Philippians 2:10). We get the privilege of willingly doing it now with other people. We should proclaim who God is with our families, our churches, at work, and everywhere we go. He is the King!

Reflection Questions

1. Have you experienced the joys of living, worshiping, and serving in community with others? What was it like?
2. Have you ever been overwhelmed with Jesus' compassion for a person or group of people? What did you do as a result?

Lord, I thank you for the privilege of worshiping you in community with other people. I am grateful that you are compassionate and close to us when we are in need. Help me to proclaim your greatness to everyone around me today.

WEEK

2

DAY 1 ⬤ Disc 1 / Track 8

My Hope and Trust

In you, LORD my God, I put my trust. I trust in you; do not let me be put to shame, nor let my enemies triumph over me. No one who hopes in you will ever be put to shame, but shame will come on those who are treacherous without cause. Show me your ways, LORD, teach me your paths. Guide me in your truth and teach me, for you are God my Savior, and my hope is in you all day long. Remember, LORD, your great mercy and love, for they are from of old. Do not remember the sins of my youth and my rebellious ways; according to your love remember me, for you, LORD, are good.

PSALM 25:1-7

Do you have a hard time trusting people? Do you have a hard time trusting God? This Psalm shows the correlation between hope and trust. Often we have a hard time trusting because our hopes were crushed when someone wasn't trustworthy in the past. I have been in that place and yet I take encouragement from verse three. "No one who hopes in you will ever be put to shame". God is completely trustworthy and we can put our hope in him.

In referring to the promise and blessing of the forgiveness of sins Hebrews 10:23 says, "Let us hold unswervingly to the hope we profess, for he who promised is faithful." When we put our hope and trust in the Lord, then we can truly say with the Psalmist in verses four and five, "Show me your ways, LORD, teach me your paths. Guide me in your truth and teach me, for you are God my Savior, and my hope is in you all day long."

As we approach each day we can look to the Lord for guidance in each conversation, decision, event, and trust that he will lead us and teach us. Then we really can put our hope in the Lord "all day long". Where else would we want to put it? Like Peter said in John 6:68 "'Lord, to whom shall we go? You have the words of eternal life.'"

This portion of the Psalm ends by underscoring God's mercy and forgiveness of sins-especially the ones of our youth. This is another reason to put our hope and trust in God-he is the only one who can forgive our sins!

Reflection Questions

1. When do you find it hard to trust God?
2. What are three concerns, worries, or fears on your mind today?

Father, I am so thankful that you are completely trustworthy and I can put my hope in you. I give you all of my concerns, worries, and fears to you today knowing that you can deal with them much better than I can.

DAY 2 ✹ ⬤ Disc 1 / Track 9

No Fear

The LORD is my light and my salvation—whom shall I fear? The LORD is the stronghold of my life—of whom shall I be afraid? When the wicked advance against me to devour me, it is my enemies and my foes who will stumble and fall. Though an army besiege me, my heart will not fear; though war break out against me, even then I will be confident. One thing I ask from the LORD, this only do I seek: that I may dwell in the house of the LORD all the days of my life, to gaze on the beauty of the LORD and to seek him in his temple. For in the day of trouble he will keep me safe in his dwelling; he will hide me in the shelter of his sacred tent and set me high upon a rock. Then my head will be exalted above the enemies who surround me; at his sacred tent I will sacrifice with shouts of joy; I will sing and make music to the LORD. Hear my voice when I call, LORD; be merciful to me and answer me. My heart says of you, "Seek his face!" Your face, LORD, I will seek. Do not hide your face from me, do not turn your servant away in anger; you have been my helper. Do not reject me or forsake me, God my Savior. Though my father and mother forsake me, the LORD will receive me.

PSALM 27:1-10

What are you afraid of? Are there fears that keep you up at night? David had enemies who wanted to kill him and he had legitimate reasons to be afraid. Yet he said, "The LORD is my light and my salvation-whom shall I fear?" (v. 1). David chose to focus on God's power rather than focus on his enemies.

When I am afraid I am tempted to focus on my fears, however this Psalm reminds me that God is bigger than those fears. When I look to the Lord I can say with the Psalmist, "whom shall I fear?"

We see that David's first passion and desire in life is to be in God's presence and to look on his beauty. "One thing I ask from the LORD, this only do I seek: that I may dwell in the house of the LORD all the days of my life, to gaze on the beauty of the LORD and to seek him in his temple" (v. 4). David knew there was nothing better than being with the Lord and being in awe of his majesty and greatness. If we do that, then when trouble comes we will automatically look to him first because we have already made him our priority.

Think of the people we confide in when life gets hard. We seek out those we are close to and trust. It's the same way with the Lord- we will seek him first if we have made him our priority and have learned to trust him. We can trust that he will protect us.

There is an urgent tone in the Psalm when he says, "Hear my voice when I call, LORD; be merciful to me and answer me" (v. 7). Then in beginning of verse nine, "Do not hide your face from me, do not turn your servant away in anger;" David had developed a confidence and trust in the Lord and he knew that even if people rejected him that God would not. It was because David had made God his priority that he knew God wouldn't forsake him. Let's seek God first today so we can truly have no fear!

Reflection Questions

1. What are you afraid of these days? What would it take for you to say and believe, "Whom shall I fear?" (v. 1)
2. Do you see how dwelling in God's house, looking on his beauty, and seeking him are antidotes to fear? (v. 4) If so, list some ways you can start doing these things.

Lord, I purpose to seek you all the days of my life and look upon your beauty. As I make you the focus of my life I know that I have no reason to be afraid. Lead me today in all my ways.

DAY 3   Disc 1 / Track 10

Blessed are the Forgiven

Blessed is the one whose transgressions are forgiven, whose sins are covered. Blessed is the one whose sin the LORD does not count against them and in whose spirit is no deceit. When I kept silent, my bones wasted away through my groaning all day long. For day and night your hand was heavy on me; my strength was sapped as in the heat of summer. Then I acknowledged my sin to you and did not cover up my iniquity. I said, "I will confess my transgressions to the LORD." And you forgave the guilt of my sin. Therefore let all the faithful pray to you while you may be found; surely the rising of the mighty waters will not reach them. You are my hiding place; you will protect me from trouble and surround me with songs of deliverance. I will instruct you and teach you in the way you should go; I will counsel you with my loving eye on you. Do not be like the horse or the mule, which have no understanding but must be controlled by bit and bridle or they will not come to you. Many are the woes of the wicked, but the LORD's unfailing love surrounds the one who trusts in him. Rejoice in the LORD and be glad, you righteous; sing, all you who are upright in heart!

PSALM 32:1-11

Have you ever felt so guilty about something that you couldn't think about anything else until the issue was resolved? That is what was going on in this Psalm. The writer acknowledged that he felt guilty for his sin day and night. It took his strength away and was exhausting. Then when he confessed his sin everything changed because he received God's forgiveness and the burden of his guilt was lifted.

As a child I was climbing on our spinet piano after I had been told not to. I fell and broke the wooden music stand that was attached to the piano. My parents scolded me for what I had done and moved on. They weren't going to punish me but I sat there and continued to cry until they disciplined me for my action! Then I was fine. What was I thinking?

This story illustrates the power of a conscience set free from the guilt of sin. I admit that my conscience was probably too sensitive in this case yet it's amazing how everything changed for me once the issue was resolved.

Verse seven says, "You are my hiding place; you will protect me from trouble and surround me with songs of deliverance." The Lord promises to be our protection and deliverance when we are in trouble. Although there are consequences for our sin, God is our protector and deliverer at all times. We can find refuge from our problems and strength to walk through them from the Lord.

Then we can truly rejoice as the Psalmist describes in verse eleven, "Rejoice in the LORD and be glad, you righteous; sing, all you who are upright in heart!"

Rather than holding on to our sin and shame let's keep short accounts with the Lord so we can experience the freedom of forgiveness.

Reflection Questions

1. Have you ever felt so guilty about something that you couldn't think about anything else? What did you do about it?
2. Is there any sin you need to confess to God today?

Father, I confess my sin of _____ to you today and ask that you would forgive me and cleanse me from all unrighteousness. Show me any additional steps I need to take today to keep a clear conscience before you.

DAY 4 Disc 1 / Track 11

The Great Creator

Sing joyfully to the LORD, you righteous; it is fitting for the upright to praise him. Praise the LORD with the harp; make music to him on the ten-stringed lyre. Sing to him a new song; play skillfully, and shout for joy. For the word of the LORD is right and true; he is faithful in all he does. The LORD loves righteousness and justice; the earth is full of his unfailing love. By the word of the LORD the heavens were made, their starry host by the breath of his mouth. He gathers the waters of the sea into jars; he puts the deep into storehouses. Let all the earth fear the LORD; let all the people of the world revere him. For he spoke, and it came to be; he commanded, and it stood firm. The LORD foils the plans of the nations; he thwarts the purposes of the peoples. But the plans of the LORD stand firm forever, the purposes of his heart through all generations.

PSALM 33:1-11

As a musician I am well aware of the power of music. It affects us spiritually, emotionally, and physically.

This Psalm begins with a call for God's people to sing joyfully to him and to praise him with different instruments. Verse three says, "Sing to him a new song; play skillfully, and shout for joy." Our creator wants us to use our creativity to worship him and to do it with excellence.

I had the privilege of studying Piano Performance at the Cincinnati College-Conservatory of Music for two years. During that time I practiced piano about three hours a day. I knew some people who would practice four to six hours a day. There were times when I felt a little out of my league.

However, it takes hard work, dedication, and time to be skillful at anything. In order to "play skillfully" to the Lord on a musical instrument we must make an investment of our time and energy. After all, the Lord is worthy of the best we can offer him.

The next part of this Psalm reminds us of God's creative power: "By the word of the LORD the heavens were made, their starry host by the breath of his mouth. Let all the earth fear the LORD; let all the people of the world revere him. For he spoke, and it came to be; he commanded, and it stood firm" (vv. 6, 8-9). The Lord is the great Creator who brought things into existence by his words so that we would stand in awe and worship him. He has put in us a desire to create and be creative for his glory. Genesis 1:27 says that we are made in God's image, "So God created mankind in his own image, in the image of God he created them; male and female he created them." No wonder we get such a sense of joy when we are being creative to the glory of God. That desire comes from him.

The next verses in the Psalm tell us that our Creator God's purposes and plans will be accomplished on the earth. Nations and peoples are under his sovereign power. Let's worship our Creator God today!

Reflection Questions

1. Do you enjoy creating things? If yes, what are some examples?
2. Since we are imperfect people, what value or worth is there in our creative endeavors? Have you seen God use your imperfections or weaknesses? If so, how?

Lord, I know that as your child you have put in me a desire to be creative for your glory. Help me to use the gifts and talents you have given me to that end. I pray that my life would encourage others to use their gifts for you as well.

DAY 5   Disc 1 / Track 12

Our Deliverer

I will extol the LORD at all times; his praise will always be on my lips. I will glory in the LORD; let the afflicted hear and rejoice. Glorify the LORD with me; let us exalt his name together. I sought the LORD, and he answered me; he delivered me from all my fears. Those who look to him are radiant; their faces are never covered with shame. This poor man called, and the LORD heard him; he saved him out of all his troubles. The angel of the LORD encamps around those who fear him, and he delivers them. Taste and see that the Lord is good; blessed is the one who takes refuge in him. Fear the LORD, you his holy people, for those who fear him lack nothing. The lions may grow weak and hungry, but those who seek the LORD lack no good thing. Come, my children, listen to me; I will teach you the fear of the LORD. Whoever of you loves life and desires to see many good days, keep your tongue from evil and your lips from telling lies. Turn from evil and do good; seek peace and pursue it. The eyes of the LORD are on the righteous, and his ears are attentive to their cry; but the face of the LORD is against those who do evil, to blot out their name from the earth. The righteous cry out, and the LORD hears them; he delivers them from all their troubles. The LORD is close to the brokenhearted and saves those who are crushed in spirit. The righteous person may have many troubles, but the LORD delivers him from them all;

PSALM 34:1-19

This Psalm was written when David was on the run from the Israelite King Saul and David entered Philistine territory. Out of fear of the Philistine king, David pretended to be insane and the king drove him away.[11] This was probably a low point in David's life because he felt he had to act like he was crazy to save himself. However, this Psalm tells us David understood the power of praising God at all times-especially when he was in trouble.

When we are in difficult circumstances we don't always feel like worshiping the Lord and yet it's the very thing we need to do. It takes our eyes of off our problems and focuses us on God's greatness. David speaks of God's deliverance in verses four through six, "I sought the LORD, and he answered me; he delivered me from all my fears. Those who look to him are radiant; their faces are never covered with shame. This poor man called, and the LORD heard him; he saved him out of all his troubles."

The Lord responded to David's cry for help and he does the same with us. I believe the reason that God was so responsive to David is because he had made the Lord the top priority in his life. He delighted in God first above everything else. That is why he says in verse eight, "Taste and see that the LORD is good; blessed is the one who takes refuge in him." When we put God first in our lives we will naturally run to him in times of need.

We have promises from this Psalm that God will help us in those times. "...those who seek the LORD lack no good thing" (v. 10). "The righteous cry out, and the LORD hears them; he delivers them from all their troubles" (v. 17). "The LORD is close to the brokenhearted and saves those who are crushed in spirit" (v. 18).

These verses tell us that God provides for us when we seek him. Matthew 6:33 says, "But seek first his kingdom and his righteousness, and all these things will be given to you as well." We also see that God listens and delivers the righteous so we should keep ourselves pure before him. Lastly we see that the Lord cares and helps those who are depressed and in emotional distress so we can go to him when our hearts are broken. Jesus said in Matthew 11:28, "Come to me, all you who are weary and burdened, and I will give you rest." He is the great deliverer so let's go to him today when we are in need.

Reflection Questions
1. Has the Lord delivered you from troubled times? If so, what was one of those times?
2. Is it hard for you to praise God when you are in difficult situations? If so, what would help you worship in those times?

Lord, I seek you today asking for help in my troubles. You say that you are "close to the brokenhearted" so I ask that you would be near to me in my brokenness and deliver me.

DAY 6 Disc 1 / Track 13

Don't Envy the Wicked

Do not fret because of those who are evil or be envious of those who do wrong; for like the grass they will soon wither, like green plants they will soon die away. Trust in the LORD and do good; dwell in the land and enjoy safe pasture. Take delight in the LORD, and he will give you the desires of your heart. Commit your way to the LORD; trust in him and he will do this: He will make your righteous reward shine like the dawn, your vindication like the noonday sun. Be still before the LORD and wait patiently for him; do not fret when people succeed in their ways, when they carry out their wicked schemes. Refrain from anger and turn from wrath; do not fret—it leads only to evil. For those who are evil will be destroyed, but those who hope in the LORD will inherit the land. A little while, and the wicked will be no more; though you look for them, they will not be found. But the meek will inherit the land and enjoy peace and prosperity. The wicked plot against the righteous and gnash their teeth at them; but the LORD laughs at the wicked, for he knows their day is coming. The wicked draw the sword and bend the bow to bring down the poor and needy, to slay those whose ways are upright. But their swords will pierce their own hearts, and their bows will be broken. Better the little that the righteous have than the wealth of many wicked; for the power of the wicked will be broken, but the LORD upholds the righteous. The LORD makes firm the steps of the one who delights in him;

PSALM 37:1-17, 23

Do you ever feel envious towards those who do not follow the Lord? We can be jealous of their apparent success despite their evil ways. This Psalm makes it very clear that things do not end well for the wicked. It clearly says, "...they will soon die away" (v. 2). "But their swords will pierce their own hearts, and their bows will be broken"

(v. 15). We are encouraged to trust in the Lord and follow in his ways.

Verse four says, "Take delight in the LORD, and he will give you the desires of your heart." As we learn to delight in the Lord he puts desires in our hearts and he fulfills them. God does want to bless us.

We are commanded to, "Be still before the LORD and wait patiently for him" (v. 7). These are characteristics of someone who follows God. Being still before God goes against the busy pace that is encouraged in our culture and yet it is so important for us. How can we be patient if we are always in a hurry?

Verse eight says, "Refrain from anger and turn from wrath; do not fret-it leads only to evil." After this command to avoid anger it is interesting that we are told not to worry because it leads to sin. How often is this true in our lives? I tend to be a worrier and yet I have seen time and again how worry does not bring me closer to God but further away. When I worry about something I am not trusting God and I am elevating the worry above God and his power. Worry can also lead to other sins like anger, revenge, etc. It is far better to trust that God will take care of every situation in our lives.

This Psalm reminds us that God blesses and protects those who follow him. Verse twenty-three tells us there is a blessing for those who delight in him.

Reflection Questions

1. Do you ever feel jealous of wicked people? Does this Psalm give you a different perspective on evildoers?

2. Have you seen impatience, anger, and worry cause trouble in your life? (vv. 7-8) If so, how can delighting in the Lord help you change?

Father, forgive me for envying wicked people. Help me to delight myself in you and to yield my worries to you today. I trust that you will take care of every situation in my life and in the lives of those I love.

DAY 7 ● Disc 1 / Track 14

A New Song

I waited patiently for the LORD; he turned to me and heard my cry. He lifted me out of the slimy pit, out of the mud and mire; he set my feet on a rock and gave me a firm place to stand. He put a new song in my mouth, a hymn of praise to our God. Many will see and fear the LORD and put their trust in him. Blessed is the one who trusts in the LORD, who does not look to the proud, to those who turn aside to false gods. Many, LORD my God, are the wonders you have done, the things you planned for us. None can compare with you; were I to speak and tell of your deeds, they would be too many to declare. Sacrifice and offering you did not desire—but my ears you have opened—burnt offerings and sin offerings you did not require. Then I said, "Here I am, I have come— it is written about me in the scroll. I desire to do your will, my God; your law is within my heart." I proclaim your saving acts in the great assembly; I do not seal my lips, LORD, as you know. I do not hide your righteousness in my heart; I speak of your faithfulness and your saving help. I do not conceal your love and your faithfulness from the great assembly. Do not withhold your mercy from me, LORD; may your love and faithfulness always protect me.

PSALM 40:1-11

I love hearing a good song for the first time. It instantly makes me want to hear it again. A new song can teach truth, grab one's attention, or say something in a different way. Many times when I hear a song for the first time it speaks to me about something going on in my life.

I have also had the privilege of writing some songs about things God has done in my life. This is exactly what this Psalm is about.

David called out to the Lord in his troubles and God helped him. Then he says, "...he set my feet on a rock and gave me a firm place to stand" (v. 2). God made things secure and stable for David. Then he put a new song in David's mouth that became a testimony to others. "Many will see and fear the Lord and put their trust in him" (v. 3).

You do not have to write songs to have God put a new song in your mouth. Sometimes it is a song someone else wrote and other times I think the song is your life. When God does something amazing in our lives we cannot help but tell others about what he has done!

In verse six the Psalmist reminds us that God is interested in our hearts more than sacrifices, "Sacrifice and offering you did not desire-but my ears you have opened-burnt offerings and sin offerings you did not require." This verse is probably a reference to the custom a servant went through in boring his ear to pledge his allegiance to his master. It could also mean that God had "opened" his ears.[12] Either way it signifies devotion to the Lord. He wanted to please the Lord and God's law was in his heart.

Then he proclaimed it in the presence of others. Let's let the new song that God puts in our hearts today come out so others will "put their trust in the Lord".

Reflection Questions

1. Has God ever put a "new song" in your mouth? What kind of a song was it?

2. Has someone ever been helped or encouraged by your testimony of something God did in your life? If so, what happened?

Lord, put a new song in my mouth today that gives you glory for the things you have done in my life. Let others hear it and turn to you as a result.

WEEK

3

DAY 1   Disc 1 / Track 15

My Soul Longs for God

As the deer pants for streams of water, so my soul pants for you, my God. My soul thirsts for God, for the living God. When can I go and meet with God? My tears have been my food day and night, while people say to me all day long, "Where is your God?" These things I remember as I pour out my soul: how I used to go to the house of God under the protection of the Mighty One with shouts of joy and praise among the festive throng. Why, my soul, are you downcast? Why so disturbed within me? Put your hope in God, for I will yet praise him, my Savior and my God. My soul is downcast within me; therefore I will remember you from the land of the Jordan, the heights of Hermon—from Mount Mizar. Deep calls to deep in the roar of your waterfalls; all your waves and breakers have swept over me. By day the Lord directs his love, at night his song is with me— a prayer to the God of my life. I say to God my Rock, "Why have you forgotten me? Why must I go about mourning, oppressed by the enemy?" My bones suffer mortal agony as my foes taunt me, saying to me all day long, "Where is your God?" Why, my soul, are you downcast? Why so disturbed within me? Put your hope in God, for I will yet praise him, my Savior and my God.

PSALM 42:1-11

Do you remember the last time you longed for a drink of water? Maybe you were on a hike, taking a run, or just outside all day in the warm weather. This is the longing that is expressed at the start of this Psalm. The Psalmist is longing to spend time in God's presence and to be with him. Life has been hard, full of tears, and those around him are questioning whether God will help him or not.

He remembers when things were good and he led others in worship of God. At the moment he is depressed and he tells himself to put his "hope in God". This kind of talking to one's self is a good thing. He says, "Put your hope in God, for I will yet praise him, my Savior and my God" (v. 5). He decides to worship the Lord in the middle of his pain and misery.

This is a great lesson for us. Worship of God is not an activity reserved for the times when we feel like doing it. It is essential for us to do at all times. Sometimes when I am filled with anxiety I just have to trust that things will get better because the Lord has been faithful to me in the past.

It is amazing how a good night's sleep can really help things. It doesn't always take the problem away but I think we underestimate the power of sleep, diet, exercise, and how it affects us. I think being wise in those areas of our lives is a way to "put our hope in God".

The beginning of verse eight reminds us that God is always working and watching over us even when we sleep. "By day the LORD directs his love, at night his song is with me".

The end of the Psalm contains a prayer reiterating a cry for help. "I say to God my Rock, 'Why have you forgotten me?'" (v. 9). I find it interesting that even at a point of desperation the author refers to God as his Rock. He knows God is the only one who can truly help him and so he says to himself again, "Put your hope in God, for I will yet praise him, my Savior and my God" (v. 11). Let's allow our problems to create a greater longing in our hearts for the Lord knowing that our hope will be increased as we praise him.

Reflection Questions

1. Have you ever experienced a longing for God like a craving for a drink of water? What was it like?

2. How do sleep, diet, and exercise affect you emotionally and spiritually?

Father, I put my hope in you today. I want my problems to create a greater longing in my heart for you. By God's grace I choose to give you all my worries and anxieties today.

DAY 2 · Disc 1 / Track 16

The Dwelling of the Most High

God is our refuge and strength, an ever-present help in trouble. Therefore we will not fear, though the earth give way and the mountains fall into the heart of the sea, though its waters roar and foam and the mountains quake with their surging. There is a river whose streams make glad the city of God, the holy place where the Most High dwells. God is within her, she will not fall; God will help her at break of day. Nations are in uproar, kingdoms fall; he lifts his voice, the earth melts. The LORD Almighty is with us; the God of Jacob is our fortress. Come and see what the LORD has done, the desolations he has brought on the earth. He makes wars cease to the ends of the earth. He breaks the bow and shatters the spear; he burns the shields with fire. He says, "Be still, and know that I am God; I will be exalted among the nations, I will be exalted in the earth." The LORD Almighty is with us; the God of Jacob is our fortress.

PSALM 46:1-11

This Psalm begins by stating that God is our refuge and strength in troubled times. No matter what happens around us we do not have to be afraid.

Then it says, "There is a river whose streams make glad the city of God, the holy place where the Most High dwells" (v. 4). There is something powerful about the presence of God where the Most High dwells. Scripture contains many references to God's presence and people who sought after it.

Moses was so adamant that God's presence be with him and the Israelites that he said, "'If your presence does not go with us do not send us up from here. How will anyone know that you are pleased with me and with your people unless you go with us? What else will distinguish me and your people from all the other people on the face of the earth?'" (Exodus 33:15-16). The Lord's presence shows that his favor is on his people and it sets them apart. Do people know that we love the Lord and seek to serve him? There is security in knowing that God is with us. "The LORD Almighty is with us; the God of Jacob is our fortress" (v. 7).

If we are followers of Jesus we have the indwelling Spirit of God within us but there is something powerful about the manifest presence of God. There are times when God shows his presence to us very clearly at a church service, in a conversation, on a mission trip, etc. The Holy Spirit can lead us to say something to a co-worker or to just stop and pray for someone when we are at home. It is in these times that we are reminded just how amazing and powerful God's presence is and that we need to be seeking it all of the time. Let's seek God's presence today!

Reflection Questions

1. Have you experienced God's manifest presence? What was it like?
2. Does the Lord's presence distinguish you from those around you? If so, how?

Lord, make me more aware of your presence today. I love to be in your presence and it changes me. Let others see you working in my life as a result of my spending time with you.

DAY 3   Disc 1 / Track 17

Make Some Noise

Clap your hands, all you nations; shout to God with cries of joy. For the LORD Most High is awesome, the great King over all the earth. He subdued nations under us, peoples under our feet. He chose our inheritance for us, the pride of Jacob, whom he loved. God has ascended amid shouts of joy, the LORD amid the sounding of trumpets. Sing praises to God, sing praises; sing praises to our King, sing praises. For God is the King of all the earth; sing to him a psalm of praise. God reigns over the nations; God is seated on his holy throne. The nobles of the nations assemble as the people of the God of Abraham, for the kings of the earth belong to God; he is greatly exalted.

PSALM 47:1-9

There is a time and place for great celebration! I remember when the Seattle Seahawks football team won the Super Bowl in 2014. Our city celebrated for weeks after that-as they should have. However, it always amazes me how people can get so excited about a ball made of leather and yet not worship the Lord with the same enthusiasm.

When we truly get a glimpse of the greatness of the Lord there are times when we just have to make some noise. We clap our hands, shout to God, and proclaim how awesome he is.

As an earthly king or ruler is applauded, how much more should we applaud and honor our heavenly king. Earthly rulers are full of inadequacies, weaknesses, and sins, and yet our heavenly Father should be worshiped in all of his perfection. He is truly glorious and he rules over the entire earth. "Sing praises to God, sing praises; sing praises to our King, sing praises. For God is the King of all the earth; sing to him a psalm of praise. God reigns over the nations; God is seated on his holy throne" (vv. 6-8).

Although Satan has been given a limited amount of authority here on this earth now, there is a time coming when the Lord will rule completely. Revelation twenty-one speaks of the new heaven and new earth where God will rule in the fullness of his power. I look forward to that day but I don't need to wait until then to worship the Lord the way he deserves. He always has been and always will be worthy of all worship and praise.

This Psalm highlights God's faithfulness to his chosen people Israel and yet scripture makes it clear that the way has been opened for Gentiles to be his people as well. "...even us, whom he also called, not only from the Jews but also from the Gentiles? As he says in Hosea: 'I will call them 'my people' who are not my people; and I will call her 'my loved one' who is not my loved one'" (Rom. 9:24-25). Because of Jesus' death and resurrection, we can become children of God. This is another reason to loudly praise God!

Reflection Questions

1. When do you like to make lots of noise? Are you comfortable "making noise" for the Lord?

2. How could you be more expressive in formal worship?

Lord, I rejoice that you have made me your child. I love to clap my hands and shout for joy to tell others of your greatness. Give me the boldness to make noise for you when the time is right.

DAY 4 Disc 1 / Track 18

Have Mercy on Me

Have mercy on me, O God, according to your unfailing love; according to your great compassion blot out my transgressions. Wash away all my iniquity and cleanse me from my sin. For I know my transgressions, and my sin is always before me. Against you, you only, have I sinned and done what is evil in your sight; so you are right in your verdict and justified when you judge. Surely I was sinful at birth, sinful from the time my mother conceived me. Yet you desired faithfulness even in the womb; you taught me wisdom in that secret place. Cleanse me with hyssop, and I will be clean; wash me, and I will be whiter than snow. Let me hear joy and gladness; let the bones you have crushed rejoice. Hide your face from my sins and blot out all my iniquity. Create in me a pure heart, O God, and renew a steadfast spirit within me. Do not cast me from your presence or take your Holy Spirit from me. Restore to me the joy of your salvation and grant me a willing spirit, to sustain me. Then I will teach transgressors your ways, so that sinners will turn back to you. Deliver me from the guilt of bloodshed, O God, you who are God my Savior, and my tongue will sing of your righteousness. Open my lips, LORD, and my mouth will declare your praise. You do not delight in sacrifice, or I would bring it; you do not take pleasure in burnt offerings. My sacrifice, O God, is a broken spirit; a broken and contrite heart you, God, will not despise. May it please you to prosper Zion, to build up the walls of Jerusalem. Then you will delight in the sacrifices of the righteous, in burnt offerings offered whole; then bulls will be offered on your altar.

PSALM 51:1-19

This famous Psalm was written when Nathan the prophet came and confronted David about committing adultery with Bathsheba. These verses have encouraged many Christians in dealing with their own sins.

David asks for mercy and forgiveness from God. He admits that what he did was wrong and that ultimately his sin is against God alone even though it affected others. He asks God to cleanse him. There is a longing in this Psalm for David to experience joy, gladness, and a right relationship with God again. He says, "Create in me a pure heart, O God, and renew a steadfast spirit within me. Do not cast me from your presence or take your Holy Spirit from me. Restore to me the joy of your salvation and grant me a willing spirit, to sustain me. Then I will teach transgressors your ways, so that sinners will turn back to you" (vv. 10-13).

I have always respected and appreciated David's heart for the Lord. He was called a man after God's heart.[13] His heart was tender to the Lord and he sought after God. Even though he committed great sins he did repent when he needed to. He valued God's presence and wanted to remain close to the Lord after he had committed these sins.

David wanted to proclaim God's greatness to others again and he knew that God wanted his heart more than sacrifices. "You do not delight in sacrifice, or I would bring it; you do not take pleasure in burnt offerings. My sacrifice, O God, is a broken spirit; a broken and contrite heart you, God, will not despise" (vv. 16-17). David was broken before the Lord and he knew that God would forgive him and restore him. I want to have a heart like David's that seeks after God, admits when I am wrong, and seeks to be restored to the Lord when needed.

Reflection Questions

1. Do you have a hard time admitting when you are wrong? Why or why not?

2. When you sin, are you more concerned with restoring your relationship with the Lord or with not getting caught/punished? How can you place more value on your relationship with God?

Father, have mercy on me for my sins. Forgive me for wrong thoughts, words, attitudes, and actions. Give me a heart like David's who valued his relationship with you above all else.

DAY 5   Disc 1 / Track 19

Vindicate Me

Save me, O God, by your name; vindicate me by your might. Hear my prayer, O God; listen to the words of my mouth. Arrogant foes are attacking me; ruthless people are trying to kill me—people without regard for God. Surely God is my help; the Lord is the one who sustains me. Let evil recoil on those who slander me; in your faithfulness destroy them. I will sacrifice a freewill offering to you; I will praise your name, LORD, for it is good. You have delivered me from all my troubles, and my eyes have looked in triumph on my foes.

PSALM 54:1-7

I don't know anyone who likes being blamed for something they did not do. False accusations can be the breeding ground for frustration, anger, fear, anxiety, and other negative emotions.

This Psalm was written when King Saul and 3,000 of his soldiers were hunting David down to kill him. It was Saul's jealousy that had caused him to turn against David. The Lord had turned against Saul because of his disobedience and the prophet Samuel had anointed David to be the next King of Israel.

However, David's time to rule had not yet come. In this Psalm, David asks God to save him and to vindicate him. There comes a time when we cannot fight our own battles. We need the Lord to justify our case and to present us blameless before others.

David knew that Saul was in the wrong but when the king wants you dead there is not much you can do except run. David says, "Arrogant foes are attacking me; ruthless people are trying to kill me-people without regard for God. Surely God is my help; the LORD is the one who sustains me" (vv. 3-4). King Saul and his men were after

David but others may have been chasing David too.[14] David looks to the Lord for help and strength on this long journey of fleeing. He calls on God to destroy his enemies and then he begins to worship the Lord. "I will praise your name, LORD, for it is good" (v. 6).

The next time we are tempted to fight our own battles we need to remember to let God vindicate us. He can defend us better than any earthly lawyer. He is our defense!

Reflection Questions

1. Have you ever been falsely accused? How did you handle the situation?
2. How can you let God "fight your battles" or defend you?

Lord, I yield the right to defend myself to you. You are my defense and my protector. I look to you for help and strength each day. When I am wrongly accused, remind me to worship and praise you as I wait for your vindication.

DAY 6   Disc 1 / Track 20

Be Exalted O God

Have mercy on me, my God, have mercy on me, for in you I take refuge. I will take refuge in the shadow of your wings until the disaster has passed. I cry out to God Most High, to God, who vindicates me. He sends from heaven and saves me, rebuking those who hotly pursue me—God sends forth his love and his faithfulness. I am in the midst of lions; I am forced to dwell among ravenous beasts—men whose teeth are spears and arrows, whose tongues are sharp swords. Be exalted, O God, above the heavens; let your glory be over all the earth. They spread a net for my feet—I was bowed down in distress. They dug a pit in my path—but they have fallen into it themselves. My heart, O God, is steadfast, my heart is steadfast; I will sing and make music. Awake, my soul! Awake, harp and lyre! I will awaken the dawn. I will praise you, Lord, among the nations; I will sing of you among the peoples. For great is your love, reaching to the heavens; your faithfulness reaches to the skies. Be exalted, O God, above the heavens; let your glory be over all the earth.

PSALM 57:1-11

David was hiding in a cave from King Saul when he wrote this Psalm. He looks to God for his protection and safety. He compares his pursuers to animals whose teeth and tongues are weapons of destruction. Not only were they trying to kill him but they were probably slandering him as well.[15]

Then he says, "Be exalted, O God, above the heavens; let your glory be over all the earth" (v. 5). In the middle of David's hiding out he begins to worship the Lord and he acknowledges God's glory in the heavens and on the earth. What an example for us. When we are being attacked, we should stop and acknowledge God's glory being over everything-including our enemies. The Psalmist's enemies had set a trap for David only they got caught in the trap themselves.

Verse seven says, "My heart, O God, is steadfast, my heart is steadfast; I will sing and make music." David was devoted to God and specifically to praising God at all times. How can we be faithful to God when we don't feel like it? The answer is in this Psalm. "...your (God's) faithfulness reaches to the skies" (v. 10). We can be faithful to God because he is faithful and he empowers us to be as well. Hebrews 10:23 says, "Let us hold unswervingly to the hope we profess, for he who promised is faithful."

The Lord is more concerned with our faithfulness than with our giftedness. In other words, we don't have to be the smartest, richest, or most talented. We simply need to be faithful with what we have been given.

David ends the Psalm by saying again, "Be exalted, O God, above the heavens; let your glory be over all the earth" (v. 11).

Reflection Questions

1. How can focusing on God's glory help you when you are attacked?

2. Is God more concerned with your faithfulness to him or your talents, riches, and intelligence? In what ways would you like to be more faithful to the Lord?

Lord, I desire to be faithful to you and to exalt you at all times-especially when I am under attack. Help me to be faithful to you with the talents and opportunities you give me.

DAY 7 Disc 1 / Track 21

My Soul Finds Rest in God

Truly my soul finds rest in God; my salvation comes from him. Truly he is my rock and my salvation; he is my fortress, I will never be shaken. How long will you assault me? Would all of you throw me down—this leaning wall, this tottering fence? Surely they intend to topple me from my lofty place; they take delight in lies. With their mouths they bless, but in their hearts they curse. Yes, my soul, find rest in God; my hope comes from him. Truly he is my rock and my salvation; he is my fortress, I will not be shaken. My salvation and my honor depend on God; he is my mighty rock, my refuge. Trust in him at all times, you people; pour out your hearts to him, for God is our refuge.

PSALM 62:1-8

In the summer of 2014 I took a sabbatical from my ministry as a pastor. It was a wonderful time of rest and refreshment based on God's example of resting on the seventh day after creating the heavens and the earth. "Then God blessed the seventh day and made it holy, because on it he rested from all the work of creating that he had done" (Genesis 2:3).

My passion for God, my family, and my ministry was renewed. I found that time in God's Word and worship of him filled me up like nothing else during the sabbatical.

David begins this Psalm by saying, "Truly my soul finds rest in God; my salvation comes from him. Truly he is my rock and my salvation; he is my fortress, I will never be shaken" (vv. 1-2). Ultimately only God can give us the rest and protection we need. We can run to other things, but they will not deliver us.

Many times we seek out entertainment as a diversion when we are faced with problems. Although those things can be good they will not renew us like the Lord and his Word can.

The author mentions enemies who are attacking him, lying about him, and possibly trying to steal his kingdom from him. He chooses to look to God for his rest, hope, protection, and salvation. God was his rock and his trust was in him.

As I began my sabbatical I found that I had allowed the pressures of life to drain me of my passion. As I began to write these Psalm devotionals I found great encouragement, strength, and hope from how God delivered David time and again. I realized that most of the Psalms were written in a time of trial, temptation, or great need. This is where we too often find ourselves. Then as I began to write accompanying piano pieces to these devotionals I found that the Psalms and the writing of the music brought me peace. This has helped me to affirm my rest in God alone.

Have you learned to find your rest in God alone? Are you frantically searching for peace in places where it ultimately cannot be found? Philippians 4:6-7 says, "Do not be anxious about anything, but in every situation, by prayer and petition, with thanksgiving, present your requests to God. And the peace of God, which transcends all understanding, will guard your hearts and your minds in Christ Jesus." The promise for us is that if we go to God with our concerns and needs in prayer that his peace will guard our hearts and minds and we will find rest in him.

Reflection Questions

1. What does David mean when he says, "My soul finds rest in God alone"? (v. 1)
2. What activities bring you rest and spiritual refreshment?

Lord, I confess that I often run to the wrong places to find peace in life. I know that my rest can only be found in you. Today I give you my problems, concerns, cares, and I trust your promise that you will guard my heart and mind with your peace.

WEEK

4

DAY 1 Disc 1 / Track 22

Your Love is Better than Life

You, God, are my God, earnestly I seek you; I thirst for you, my whole being longs for you, in a dry and parched land where there is no water. I have seen you in the sanctuary and beheld your power and your glory. Because your love is better than life, my lips will glorify you. I will praise you as long as I live, and in your name I will lift up my hands. I will be fully satisfied as with the richest of foods; with singing lips my mouth will praise you. On my bed I remember you; I think of you through the watches of the night. Because you are my help, I sing in the shadow of your wings. I cling to you; your right hand upholds me. Those who want to kill me will be destroyed; they will go down to the depths of the earth. They will be given over to the sword and become food for jackals. But the king will rejoice in God; all who swear by God will glory in him, while the mouths of liars will be silenced.

PSALM 63:1-11

This Psalm was written while David was in the desert of Judah probably on the run from King Saul again. He expresses an urgent longing for the Lord because he is in great distress.

David knows how great and glorious God is because he has been in the sanctuary and seen what the Lord has done in the past. He says, "Because your love is better than life, my lips will glorify you. I will praise you as long as I live, and in your name I will lift up my hands. I will be fully satisfied as with the richest of foods; with singing lips my mouth will praise you" (vv. 3-5). David knows that God's love is better than anything this life has to offer so he worships the Lord and seeks to be satisfied in him. This is a great truth for us today.

Do we truly believe that God's "love is better than life"? If we do, then it will be reflected in our worship of him. As we are satisfied by rich foods so we need to be spiritually filled up by God. However our tendency is to look for fulfillment first in relationships, sports, food, money, etc. John Piper addresses this in his book *Desiring God*. When we look to these things before God we will never be satisfied. Yet when we look to God first and then put other things in their proper place we will be satisfied.[16] Deuteronomy 5:9 says, "You shall not bow down to them or worship them; for I, the LORD your God, am a jealous God".

I am amazed at how often I can get frustrated or out of sorts when things don't go my way during the day. In those moments I am forgetting that God is my source of joy and nothing can take his love away from me. As Romans 8:38-39 says, "For I am convinced that neither death nor life, neither angels nor demons, neither the present nor the future, nor any powers, neither height nor depth, nor anything else in all creation, will be able to separate us from the love of God that is in Christ Jesus our Lord."

The Psalm goes on to say that David thinks about God during the night and he looks to the Lord for his deliverance. He believes that God will destroy his enemies and he chooses to rejoice in God. If we learn to value the Lord and his love as better than anything this life has to offer we can do the same!

Reflection Questions

1. Have you experienced God's love as "better than life"? (v. 3)
2. How can believing God's love is "better than life" help you with your daily frustrations and struggles?

Father I know your love is better than life so help me to live like that is true. I want my thoughts, words, and actions to reflect a steady trust in your love for me. In times of trouble help me to look to you first for my joy and satisfaction.

DAY 2   Disc 1 / Track 23

A Blessing From the Lord

*May God be gracious to us and bless us and make his face shine on us—
so that your ways may be known on earth, your salvation among all nations. May the peoples praise you, God; may all the peoples praise you.
May the nations be glad and sing for joy, for you rule the peoples with
equity and guide the nations of the earth. May the peoples praise you,
God; may all the peoples praise you. The land yields its harvest; God, our
God, blesses us. May God bless us still, so that all the ends of the earth
will fear him.*

PSALM 67:1-7

Have you experienced the power of a blessing in your life? Words
of blessing can change our outlook, encourage us, and redirect our
steps.

The first verse of this Psalm is taken from this blessing in Num-
bers 6:24-26, "The LORD bless you and keep you; the LORD make
his face shine on you and be gracious to you; the LORD turn his face
toward you and give you peace."

My father would often say this blessing over me at night before
bed and we often say it to our boys as well. What an amazing promise that the Lord of all creation would bless us and make his glorious
face shine on us. This Psalm says that God does this so that people
will come to know him and his greatness, and that they would worship him.

Are you speaking blessings over your family, friends, and those
you come in contact with every day? You don't have to say a formal blessing. Often a blessing comes in the form of an encouraging
word, note, or email. How often do we compliment people with no

ulterior motives? In other words, do we bless people simply for their good? Encouraging words people have spoken to me have given me strength in difficult seasons of my life. Just think of how we can do that for others.

The Psalm ends by reiterating that God's blessings will cause the nations to know, honor, and respect him. "May God bless us still, so that all the ends of the earth will fear him" (v. 7). Go speak a blessing over someone today!

Reflection Questions

1. Has someone spoken words of blessing to you that impacted you greatly? What was the result?
2. Who might the Lord want you to speak words of blessing to this week?

Thank you Lord for blessing my life. I pray that you would make your face shine on me today so that I can be a blessing to others and point them to you.

DAY 3 Disc 1 / Track 24

All My Life and All Day Long

In you, LORD, I have taken refuge; let me never be put to shame. In your righteousness, rescue me and deliver me; turn your ear to me and save me. Be my rock of refuge, to which I can always go; give the command to save me, for you are my rock and my fortress. Deliver me, my God, from the hand of the wicked, from the grasp of those who are evil and cruel. For you have been my hope, Sovereign LORD, my confidence since my youth. From birth I have relied on you; you brought me forth from my mother's womb. I will ever praise you. I have become a sign to many; you are my strong refuge. My mouth is filled with your praise, declaring your splendor all day long. Do not cast me away when I am old; do not forsake me when my strength is gone. For my enemies speak against me; those who wait to kill me conspire together. They say, "God has forsaken him; pursue him and seize him, for no one will rescue him." Do not be far from me, my God; come quickly, God, to help me. May my accusers perish in shame; may those who want to harm me be covered with scorn and disgrace. As for me, I will always have hope; I will praise you more and more. My mouth will tell of your righteous deeds, of your saving acts all day long—though I know not how to relate them all. I will come and proclaim your mighty acts, Sovereign LORD; I will proclaim your righteous deeds, yours alone. Since my youth, God, you have taught me, and to this day I declare your marvelous deeds. Even when I am old and gray, do not forsake me, my God, till I declare your power to the next generation, your mighty acts to all who are to come. Your righteousness, God, reaches to the heavens, you who have done great things. Who is like you, God? Though you have made me see troubles, many and bitter, you will restore my life again; from the depths of the earth you will again bring me up.

You will increase my honor and comfort me once more. I will praise you with the harp for your faithfulness, my God; I will sing praise to you with the lyre, Holy One of Israel. My lips will shout for joy when I sing praise to you—I whom you have delivered. My tongue will tell of your righteous acts all day long, for those who wanted to harm me have been put to shame and confusion.

PSALM 71:1-24

This Psalm is a cry for protection and help from God. David is again asking for deliverance from his enemies. He says that the Lord has been his hope and confidence since he was young.

There is a great lesson for us in those two words. Is God truly our hope and confidence? Do we put our confidence in our education, talents, finances, or our accomplishments? Those things will disappoint us at some point. Putting our confidence in God and his Word is a solid foundation.

Is our hope in the things of this life or in the Lord? As Proverbs 13:12 says, "Hope deferred makes the heart sick, but a longing fulfilled is a tree of life." Only the Lord can fulfill our deepest longings and hopes.

Then the Psalmist takes things a step further in verse six, "From birth I have relied on you; you brought me forth from my mother's womb. I will ever praise you." David is saying that he has been dependent on God from the moment he was brought into the world. He is praising the Lord because every breath he takes is from God.

Then he says, "My mouth is filled with your praise, declaring your splendor all day long" (v. 8). David decides to worship God all day long. The God who has watched over him from birth is worthy of praise every moment of the day. Do we take time to worship God throughout the day or just during our prayer and reading of the Bible? This can happen by simply thanking God for his blessings throughout the day.

He mentions God's faithfulness again in verses seventeen and eighteen, "Since my youth, God, you have taught me, and to this day I declare your marvelous deeds. Even when I am old and gray, do not forsake me, my God, till I declare your power to the next generation, your mighty acts to all who are to come." We need to be declaring God's awesome deeds all the time. When we are old we get the privilege of telling the next generation of God's faithfulness and power. This is an encouraging thought! The elderly have a calling and mission statement to declare the greatness of God to the younger generations. We can look forward to teaching, challenging, and encouraging the younger generations even more when we get older.

I love learning from the wisdom of those older than me. The pastors, piano teachers, and other people the Lord has put in my path have helped me in times of great need. What a privilege to learn from their experience and how God has taught and used them. Since God has been faithful to us our whole life long let's make sure we worship him all day long!

Reflection Questions

1. Do you have any examples of how the Lord has watched over you from your birth?
2. Do you take time to worship the Lord throughout the day? If not, how can you remind yourself to do that?

Father, I am truly grateful for your faithfulness to me throughout my life. I want to be faithful to worship you all day long. I put my confidence and hope in you today.

DAY 4 Disc 1 / Track 25

Boast No More

We praise you, God, we praise you, for your Name is near; people tell of your wonderful deeds. You say, "I choose the appointed time; it is I who judge with equity. When the earth and all its people quake, it is I who hold its pillars firm. To the arrogant I say, 'Boast no more,' and to the wicked, 'Do not lift up your horns. Do not lift your horns against heaven; do not speak so defiantly.'" No one from the east or the west or from the desert can exalt themselves. It is God who judges: He brings one down, he exalts another. In the hand of the LORD is a cup full of foaming wine mixed with spices; he pours it out, and all the wicked of the earth drink it down to its very dregs. As for me, I will declare this forever; I will sing praise to the God of Jacob, who says, "I will cut off the horns of all the wicked, but the horns of the righteous will be lifted up."

PSALM 75:1-10

This Psalm underscores God's role as righteous judge of the earth. It begins with gratitude to God for his powerful presence and for his mighty deeds. Nations and peoples may not acknowledge the Lord but he is firmly in control. God said, "When the earth and all its people quake, it is I who hold its pillars firm. To the arrogant I say, 'Boast no more,' and to the wicked, 'Do not lift up your horns'" (vv. 3-4). This is a great reminder that no matter what tragedies and evils happen on this earth, God holds this world firmly in his hand.

Realizing that we really don't have any control is an antidote against pride and boasting. Pride can come into our lives so subtly. It can start with a desire for excellence that turns into boasting or when given privilege or power we can become self-dependent. Verses six and seven say, "No one from the east or the west or from the desert can exalt themselves. It is God who judges: He brings one down, he exalts another." God lifts men up and brings them down. I Pet. 5:6 says, "Humble yourselves, therefore, under God's mighty hand, that he may lift you up in due time."

If God wants to give us opportunity, promote us, and bless us he will do it. We must learn to humble ourselves before him and trust that his ways are best. Learning to be content in God's ways takes away the need to put ourselves above others because we know that our worth and security are in the Lord. He is the ultimate judge of both the righteous and the wicked and he will judge the wicked. Let's humble ourselves before God today.

Reflection Questions

1. How can contentment take away our need to elevate ourselves above others?
2. When are you tempted to pride? How can acknowledging your lack of control over life's situations help?

Lord, I am thankful that you are in control of the nations and the peoples of the earth. When I am tempted to pride and boasting help me remember that you hold everything in your hands. I humble myself before your throne today knowing that only you are worthy of praise.

DAY 5   Disc 2 / Track 1

Are You Listening?

Sing for joy to God our strength; shout aloud to the God of Jacob! Begin the music, strike the timbrel, play the melodious harp and lyre. Sound the ram's horn at the New Moon, and when the moon is full, on the day of our festival; this is a decree for Israel, an ordinance of the God of Jacob. When God went out against Egypt, he established it as a statute for Joseph. I heard an unknown voice say: "I removed the burden from their shoulders; their hands were set free from the basket. In your distress you called and I rescued you, I answered you out of a thundercloud; I tested you at the waters of Meribah. Hear me, my people, and I will warn you—if you would only listen to me, Israel! You shall have no foreign god among you; you shall not worship any god other than me. I am the LORD your God, who brought you up out of Egypt. Open wide your mouth and I will fill it. "But my people would not listen to me; Israel would not submit to me. So I gave them over to their stubborn hearts to follow their own devices. "If my people would only listen to me, if Israel would only follow my ways, how quickly I would subdue their enemies and turn my hand against their foes! Those who hate the LORD would cringe before him, and their punishment would last forever. But you would be fed with the finest of wheat; with honey from the rock I would satisfy you."

PSALM 81:1-16

This Psalm begins with joyful praise to God who is our strength. We are told to sing, shout, and play instruments to the Lord.

The Psalmist references God's deliverance of the Israelites from Egyptian slavery and oppression. The Lord made the waters of the Red Sea close on the Egyptians and he provided water for them from a Rock at Meribah. Then God says, "Hear me, my people, and I will warn you-if you would only listen to me, Israel! You shall have no foreign god among you; you shall not worship any god other than me. I am the LORD your God, who brought you up out of Egypt. Open wide your mouth and I will fill it" (vv. 8-10). The Lord told his people to listen to him and to worship him alone. He had provided for their deliverance in the past and promised to continue to provide for them.

Do we listen to the Lord? There were unwanted consequences when the Israelites didn't listen to the Lord. However, he promised to conquer their enemies if they would listen to him.

Listening is so important in every relationship we have. I am amazed at how often our kids' ears perk up when my wife and I are talking about something they aren't supposed to hear. I wish we were all that attentive when listening. Truly Listening to others can diffuse an argument and being listened to can encourage our hearts when we are feeling defeated.

Listening to God is essential to happiness as a follower of Jesus. This is what God says about those who listen to him: "But you would be fed with the finest of wheat; with honey from the rock I would satisfy you" (v. 16). Those who listen to God will be provided for and they will experience joy.

The first verse of this Psalm speaks of joy and the last verse speaks of satisfaction. Listening to God is a key to experiencing both of these things. Let's tune our ears to the Lord today and listen to him!

Reflection Questions

1. How can listening to God bring joy and satisfaction to your life?
2. What steps can you take to become a better listener?

Father, I want to hear your voice today. I know that true joy and satisfaction in life come from listening to and obeying you. Help me to do that today.

DAY 6   Disc 2 / Track 2

One Day in Your Courts

How lovely is your dwelling place, LORD Almighty! My soul yearns, even faints, for the courts of the LORD; my heart and my flesh cry out for the living God. Even the sparrow has found a home, and the swallow a nest for herself, where she may have her young—a place near your altar, LORD Almighty, my King and my God. Blessed are those who dwell in your house; they are ever praising you. Blessed are those whose strength is in you, whose hearts are set on pilgrimage. As they pass through the Valley of Baka, they make it a place of springs; the autumn rains also cover it with pools. They go from strength to strength, till each appears before God in Zion. Hear my prayer, Lord God Almighty; listen to me, God of Jacob. Look on our shield, O God; look with favor on your anointed one. Better is one day in your courts than a thousand elsewhere; I would rather be a doorkeeper in the house of my God than dwell in the tents of the wicked. For the LORD God is a sun and shield; the LORD bestows favor and honor; no good thing does he withhold from those whose walk is blameless. LORD Almighty, blessed is the one who trusts in you.

PSALM 84:1-12

There are three specific blessings mentioned in this Psalm. Those who dwell in God's house, find their strength in him, and trust him will be blessed.

The first blessing is for those who love to be with the Lord. Do you long to spend time in God's presence? The Psalmist describes a longing and yearning to be with God. Verse four says, "Blessed are those who dwell in your house; they are ever praising you." When we get a picture of his greatness we cannot help but worship him.

Verse five says, "Blessed are those whose strength is in you, whose hearts are set on pilgrimage." This is the second blessing. The Israelites would travel to Jerusalem for their religious festivals.[17] In the same way, those who journey towards God spiritually and find their strength in him are blessed.

Do we consider each day part of our journey with God? If so, then we will naturally look to him for strength in each situation. Psalm 73:26 says, "My flesh and my heart may fail, but God is the strength of my heart and my portion forever." There are times in life when we get weary, tired, discouraged, and feel like giving up. What great comfort it is to know that God is the strength of our hearts-especially in those times. Our strength isn't in the economy, our relationships, or anything else on this earth.

Verse ten says, "Better is one day in your courts than a thousand elsewhere; I would rather be a doorkeeper in the house of my God than dwell in the tents of the wicked." The writer of this Psalm may have been a doorkeeper at the temple.[18] He understood that a seemingly insignificant role in God's house was many times better than following after the wicked.

Verse twelve says, "LORD Almighty, blessed is the one who trusts in you." This is the third blessing.

I remember a Christian leader in Youth With A Mission telling me in the year 2000 that I needed to learn to trust God more. Those words were spoken to me right before I got engaged to my wife Gretchen. I was trying to figure out how our relationship was going to work out. We had been dating for some time and I was going to be moving to Kansas City to continue my work with Youth With a Mission. I wanted to ask her to marry me but I was having a difficult time trusting God with the idea of us living in different cities during our engagement. Sometimes trusting means stepping out in faith even when we cannot see the outcome. After we got engaged it worked out that I was able to split my time between Kansas City and Seattle where Gretchen was until our wedding. When I stepped out in faith the Lord worked everything out. In what area of your life might God be asking you to trust him?

Reflection Questions

1. Do you love to spend time in God's presence? If so, why?
2. Do you find it easy to trust the Lord? Why or why not?

Lord, I choose to trust you today. Give me the faith to trust when I cannot see the end result. I know your ways are best and that you love me.

DAY 7   Disc 2 / Track 3

Hear My Prayer

Hear me, LORD, and answer me, for I am poor and needy. Guard my life, for I am faithful to you; save your servant who trusts in you. You are my God; have mercy on me, Lord, for I call to you all day long. Bring joy to your servant, Lord, for I put my trust in you. You, Lord, are forgiving and good, abounding in love to all who call to you. Hear my prayer, LORD; listen to my cry for mercy. When I am in distress, I call to you, because you answer me. Among the gods there is none like you, Lord; no deeds can compare with yours. All the nations you have made will come and worship before you, Lord; they will bring glory to your name. For you are great and do marvelous deeds; you alone are God. Teach me your way, LORD, that I may rely on your faithfulness; give me an undivided heart, that I may fear your name. I will praise you, Lord my God, with all my heart; I will glorify your name forever.

PSALM 86:1-12

We often have things weighing on our hearts and minds when we come to the Lord in prayer. In those moments there is great urgency in our cries for help. David writes this Psalm in one of those times. He begins by asking the Lord to hear him because he is in great need.

Then he asks for God's protection since he faithfully serves the Lord. He says, "Have mercy on me, Lord, for I call to you all day long. Bring joy to your servant, Lord, for I put my trust in you" (vv. 3-4). David asks for mercy because he calls on God all the time. When we keep short accounts with God for our failings then we can experience God's mercy all the time. When we consistently look to God in every situation he becomes the source of our joy.

Verses eight through eleven say, "Among the gods there is none like you, Lord; no deeds can compare with yours. All the nations you have made will come and worship before you, Lord; they will bring glory to your name. For you are great and do marvelous deeds; you alone are God." There is no one like the Lord. His greatness and power are beyond our comprehension. All peoples will one day worship him and give him the glory he is due. Philippians 2:10-11 says, "that at the name of Jesus every knee should bow, in heaven and on earth and under the earth, and every tongue acknowledge that Jesus Christ is Lord, to the glory of God the Father." We get the privilege to willingly bow and worship the Lord now.

Then the Psalmist asks God to teach him his ways and give him an "undivided heart" to serve him. An "undivided heart" puts God first and doesn't allow anything else to be the top priority in our lives.

Do we have an "undivided heart" that causes us to reverence, honor, and worship the Lord like we should? When this is true of us then we can worship the Lord with all our heart like the beginning of verse twelve says: "I will praise you, Lord my God, with all my heart". Then there is nothing blocking our relationship to God.

Reflection Questions
1. Have you ever cried out to God with a heavy burden? How did the Lord respond?
2. How can you develop an "undivided heart" (v. 11) towards the Lord?

Lord, hear my prayer today. I ask for help in every situation I will encouter. Help me to remember your greatness and power at all times. Give me an "undivided" heart to put you first in my life.

WEEK

5

DAY 1 ❋ 🔘 Disc 2 / Track 4

A Cry for Help

LORD, you are the God who saves me; day and night I cry out to you. May my prayer come before you; turn your ear to my cry. I am overwhelmed with troubles and my life draws near to death. I am counted among those who go down to the pit; I am like one without strength. I am set apart with the dead, like the slain who lie in the grave, whom you remember no more, who are cut off from your care. You have put me in the lowest pit, in the darkest depths. Your wrath lies heavily on me; you have overwhelmed me with all your waves. You have taken from me my closest friends and have made me repulsive to them. I am confined and cannot escape; my eyes are dim with grief. I call to you, LORD, every day; I spread out my hands to you. Do you show your wonders to the dead? Do their spirits rise up and praise you? Is your love declared in the grave, your faithfulness in Destruction? Are your wonders known in the place of darkness, or your righteous deeds in the land of oblivion? But I cry to you for help, LORD; in the morning my prayer comes before you.

PSALM 88:1-13

There are times when we are overwhelmed with trouble. In those moments we are searching for help and for something secure to hold onto. The Psalmist is in one of those times. He begins by acknowledging that God is his source of help at all times. Then he says he is close to death and is lacking strength. He feels like God has abandoned him, God's wrath is on him, and God is overwhelming him with trouble. The Psalmist's close friends have left him.

When things we have placed our hope and joy in get taken from us in life we have a choice to make. We can wallow in sadness, frustration, and fear or we can turn to the Lord for help. When we lose a job, a relationship, are faced with cancer, where do we turn?

After describing his trials the Psalmist says, "my eyes are dim with grief. I call to you, LORD, every day; I spread out my hands to you" (v. 9). He seeks the Lord's help during his troubles. Then he says, "But I cry to you for help, LORD; in the morning my prayer comes before you" (v. 13). He chooses to seek God even in the midst of great discouragement. Even when circumstances don't immediately get better in our lives we need to continue to seek God first in our lives.

James 5:16 says, "Therefore confess your sins to each other and pray for each other so that you may be healed. The prayer of a righteous person is powerful and effective." Our prayers make a difference and change things. This verse mentions our sins being forgiven. James 5:17 states that Elijah prayed that it wouldn't rain and God stopped the rain for three and a half years. Then he prayed for the rain to return and it did.

If God can choose to change the weather based on our prayers can he not alter the circumstances in our lives? He can and will according to his timetable. We simply need to be faithful in crying out to God for help and trust that he will be faithful to us.

Reflection Questions

1. Why do you think God chooses to use our prayers?
2. Have you ever turned to the Lord in a time of great sadness? What happened?

Lord, I cry out to you when life gets rough. You are the foundation of my life. When other things get taken from me help me to trust you with my whole heart. I believe you know what is best for me.

DAY 2   Disc 2 / Track 5

Stay Close to the Lord

Whoever dwells in the shelter of the Most High will rest in the shadow of the Almighty. I will say of the LORD, "He is my refuge and my fortress, my God, in whom I trust." Surely he will save you from the fowler's snare and from the deadly pestilence. He will cover you with his feathers, and under his wings you will find refuge; his faithfulness will be your shield and rampart. You will not fear the terror of night, nor the arrow that flies by day, nor the pestilence that stalks in the darkness, nor the plague that destroys at midday. A thousand may fall at your side, ten thousand at your right hand, but it will not come near you. You will only observe with your eyes and see the punishment of the wicked. If you say, "The LORD is my refuge," and you make the Most High your dwelling, no harm will overtake you, no disaster will come near your tent. For he will command his angels concerning you to guard you in all your ways; they will lift you up in their hands, so that you will not strike your foot against a stone. You will tread on the lion and the cobra; you will trample the great lion and the serpent. "Because he loves me," says the LORD, "I will rescue him; I will protect him, for he acknowledges my name. He will call on me, and I will answer him; I will be with him in trouble, I will deliver him and honor him. With long life I will satisfy him and show him my salvation."

PSALM 91:1-16

This Psalm of protection was given to me at my birth as a prayer over my life. It contains wonderful promises of protection and rest for those who seek God and stay close to him. The Lord is their help when evil and trouble are all around them.

This makes me think of our three boys. There are so many things my wife Gretchen and I do to protect them from danger. We held their hands when they were young to keep them close to us when crossing the street. We try to protect them from media, friends, and influences that will harm them spiritually.

The same is true of our heavenly Father but in much greater ways. He watches over us and protects us if we make him our treasure and focus. God's faithfulness is our shield to guard us. It says, "You will not fear the terror of night, nor the arrow that flies by day, nor the pestilence that stalks in the darkness, nor the plague that destroys at midday. A thousand may fall at your side, ten thousand at your right hand, but it will not come near you" (vv. 5-7).

We have no reason to fear when God is protecting us. People all around will be under attack and overcome and yet God's hand will keep us safe. What a promise! If we stay close to the Lord he commands angels to watch over us.

Verse fourteen says that if we love the Lord and acknowledge his name he will protect us. Those who love God will naturally worship and acknowledge him for who he is because it becomes an overflow of their heart. They will also tell others about God's goodness.

Verses fifteen and sixteen say, "He will call on me, and I will answer him; I will be with him in trouble, I will deliver him and honor him. With long life I will satisfy him and show him my salvation." The Lord promises to answer us in time of need and to help us. Those who seek the Lord will have long life and salvation. The main issue is whether or not we are staying close to the Lord. If we are, we have no reason to fear!

Reflection Questions

1. How have you seen God's protection in your life?
2. Do you feel close to the Lord these days? Why or why not?

Lord, I want to stay close to you every day. I know there is no better place for me than under your protective wings. Help me to acknowledge you in all things today.

DAY 3   Disc 2 / Track 6

Proclaim His Love and Faithfulness

It is good to praise the LORD and make music to your name, O Most High, proclaiming your love in the morning and your faithfulness at night, to the music of the ten-stringed lyre and the melody of the harp. For you make me glad by your deeds, LORD; I sing for joy at what your hands have done. How great are your works, LORD, how profound your thoughts! Senseless people do not know, fools do not understand, that though the wicked spring up like grass and all evildoers flourish, they will be destroyed forever. But you, LORD, are forever exalted. For surely your enemies, LORD, surely your enemies will perish; all evildoers will be scattered. You have exalted my horn like that of a wild ox; fine oils have been poured on me. My eyes have seen the defeat of my adversaries; my ears have heard the rout of my wicked foes. The righteous will flourish like a palm tree, they will grow like a cedar of Lebanon; planted in the house of the LORD, they will flourish in the courts of our God. They will still bear fruit in old age, they will stay fresh and green, proclaiming, "The LORD is upright; he is my Rock, and there is no wickedness in him."

PSALM 92:1-15

Some mornings I love to get up and listen to worship music as I am having my coffee and breakfast. There is something special about starting the day off with praise to the Lord. Proclaiming God's love in the morning can begin by reading and meditating on scriptures that tell of his great love for us. Then we proclaim his love in our prayers and it comes out when we are with people.

Proclaiming God's faithfulness at night begins by recalling the ways his hand guided us throughout the day and then thanking him for his provision. We also tell others about his great faithfulness.

The Psalmist actually derived his joy from recounting what the Lord had done. "For you make me glad by your deeds, LORD; I sing for joy at what your hands have done" (v. 4). When we think about the many ways the Lord watches over us, blesses us, and guides us every day we cannot help but worship him. Doing that fills us with joy in the Lord!

Wicked people don't understand that this life is not all there is. They may be successful in this life but they will perish eternally if they don't know the Lord. "The righteous will flourish like a palm tree, they will grow like a cedar of Lebanon; planted in the house of the LORD, they will flourish in the courts of our God" (vv. 12-13). The righteous will be like a tree that grows and prospers being planted in God's house.

Staying close to the Lord and to his people causes us to grow spiritually. The more we learn about God through his Word the more we want to learn. Our spiritual appetite is increased. We realize that since this life is not the end that spiritual things matter much more than physical things. Studying scripture, praying, and telling others about the Lord become more important than money, fame, and getting bigger toys when we live with heaven and eternity in view.

Reflection Questions

1. Do you take time in the evening to thank God for his faithfulness to you during the day? If so, how does it affect you?
2. How can living with eternity in view change the way we live today?

Father, I will proclaim your love today and recount your faithfulness tonight. Help me to live my life with eternity in view knowing that this life is temporary.

DAY 4   Disc 2 / Track 7

Worship and Bow Down

Come, let us sing for joy to the LORD; let us shout aloud to the Rock of our salvation. Let us come before him with thanksgiving and extol him with music and song. For the LORD is the great God, the great King above all gods. In his hand are the depths of the earth, and the mountain peaks belong to him. The sea is his, for he made it, and his hands formed the dry land. Come, let us bow down in worship, let us kneel before the LORD our Maker; for he is our God and we are the people of his pasture, the flock under his care. Today, if only you would hear his voice, "Do not harden your hearts as you did at Meribah, as you did that day at Massah in the wilderness, where your ancestors tested me; they tried me, though they had seen what I did. For forty years I was angry with that generation; I said, 'They are a people whose hearts go astray, and they have not known my ways.' So I declared on oath in my anger, 'They shall never enter my rest.'"

PSALM 95:1-11

It is a comforting thought to know that someone is watching over us. As a child, I was thankful for the adults in my life that made me feel safe and protected.

This Psalm underscores God's protection over his people whom he created like a shepherd caring for his sheep. This is the reason given for bowing down and kneeling before the Lord in worship. "Come, let us bow down in worship, let us kneel before the LORD our Maker; for he is our God and we are the people of his pasture, the flock under his care" (vv. 6-7). Like a shepherd protects his sheep from wild animals our God guards us from danger. What a great antidote to fear. We don't have to be afraid of anything in this life because our Creator is keeping watch over us.

2 Timothy 1:7 says, (NKJV) "For God has not given us a spirit of fear, but of power and of love and of a sound mind." God gives us his power, love, and his thoughts. The next time we are tempted to fear we need to ask the Lord to give us his perspective on our situation. No wonder the Psalmist calls us to bow and kneel before the Lord in worship. He will provide us with protection and all we need.

The early part of this Psalm is about singing and making music to the Lord for whom he is and what he has done. All creation is under his dominion and control.

The latter verses of the Psalm contain a warning not to harden our hearts like the Israelites did in the desert. The height of their disobedience occurred when they refused to conquer the people and land of Canaan and they paid for it with forty years of wandering in the desert. God said, "They shall never enter my rest" (v. 11). Those who were twenty years old and older (excluding Caleb and Joshua) were not able to enter the land of Canaan and they died in the desert.

The book of Hebrews explains a rest that signifies eternal life. Those who believe and follow Jesus will have their sins forgiven and enter eternal rest. The Lord wants us to trust his protection and provision. Trust today and every day for all eternity.

Reflection Questions

1. How has the Lord been like a shepherd to you in your life?
2. In what area of your life do you need to ask God to replace fear with his power, love and a sound mind? (2 Tim. 1:7)

Father, help me to trust that you are watching over and protecting me today like a shepherd guarding his sheep. I bow down and worship you today for your constant care and guidance in my life.

DAY 5   Disc 2 / Track 8

Declare His Glory

Sing to the LORD a new song; sing to the LORD, all the earth. Sing to the LORD, praise his name; proclaim his salvation day after day. Declare his glory among the nations, his marvelous deeds among all peoples. For great is the LORD and most worthy of praise; he is to be feared above all gods. For all the gods of the nations are idols, but the LORD made the heavens. Splendor and majesty are before him; strength and glory are in his sanctuary. Ascribe to the LORD, all you families of nations, ascribe to the LORD glory and strength. Ascribe to the LORD the glory due his name; bring an offering and come into his courts.

PSALM 96:1-8

The Bible contains many passages on the "glory of the Lord". This Psalm says, "Ascribe to the LORD the glory due his name; bring an offering and come into his courts" (v. 8). To bring an offering to the Lord that gives him the glory he is due we first need an understanding of how great he is.

In 1 Chronicles 29:11 King David prays, "Yours, Lord, is the greatness and the power and the glory and the majesty and the splendor, for everything in heaven and earth is yours. Yours, Lord, is the kingdom; you are exalted as head over all." David understood that since God created the heavens and the earth that his creation exemplified his greatness. However as David said, the Lord is exponentially greater than his creation as he is exalted above all.

This Psalm begins with a command to sing to the Lord and to declare his glory to all. Honor, majesty, strength, and glory (or beauty[19]) are used to describe him. His creation displays his honor and majesty. His strength and beauty are seen in his presence.

Let's put this in common terms. We can be impressed by a beautiful sunrise, the Grand Canyon, or any other natural wonder. Any majesty we see in those things is a small reflection of the honor and majesty of the Lord who made them.

We can also be impressed by the strength of great athletes or the powers of fictional super heroes. The Lord's strength and power puts them to shame. Any power we can think of someone possessing belongs to the Lord already.

An amazing by-product of giving God glory is that it changes us. 2 Corinthians 3:18 says, "And we all, who with unveiled faces contemplate the Lord's glory, are being transformed into his image with ever-increasing glory, which comes from the Lord, who is the Spirit." When we think about and focus on God's glory we become more like him. He changes our thoughts, desires, and most importantly our hearts. Let's declare his glory today!

Reflection Questions

1. Have you ever experienced the glory of the Lord? If so, how did it change you?
2. List some practical ways you can "reflect the Lord's glory" with your life. (2 Cor. 3:18)

Lord, I give you the glory you are due today. All honor, majesty, strength, and beauty are yours. Help me to reflect your glory today as you change me from the inside out.

DAY 6   Disc 2 / Track 9

Praise the Lord O my Soul

Praise the LORD, my soul; all my inmost being, praise his holy name. Praise the LORD, my soul, and forget not all his benefits—who forgives all your sins and heals all your diseases, who redeems your life from the pit and crowns you with love and compassion, who satisfies your desires with good things so that your youth is renewed like the eagle's. The LORD works righteousness and justice for all the oppressed. He made known his ways to Moses, his deeds to the people of Israel: The LORD is compassionate and gracious, slow to anger, abounding in love. He will not always accuse, nor will he harbor his anger forever; he does not treat us as our sins deserve or repay us according to our iniquities. For as high as the heavens are above the earth, so great is his love for those who fear him; as far as the east is from the west, so far has he removed our transgressions from us. As a father has compassion on his children, so the LORD has compassion on those who fear him; for he knows how we are formed, he remembers that we are dust. The life of mortals is like grass, they flourish like a flower of the field; the wind blows over it and it is gone, and its place remembers it no more. But from everlasting to everlasting the LORD's love is with those who fear him, and his righteousness with their children's children—with those who keep his covenant and remember to obey his precepts. The LORD has established his throne in heaven, and his kingdom rules over all. Praise the LORD, you his angels, you mighty ones who do his bidding, who obey his word. Praise the LORD, all his heavenly hosts, you his servants who do his will. Praise the LORD, all his works everywhere in his dominion. Praise the LORD, my soul.

PSALM 103:1-22

There are some days when I wake up and I am fighting feelings of frustration, anxiety, and discouragement. In those moments I can tell myself to choose to praise the Lord and trust him as I open up the scriptures and pray.

David begins this Psalm by telling himself to praise the Lord. He tells everything inside of him to worship the Lord. He remembers that God forgives his sins, heals his body, saves him from trouble, and gives him love and compassion. Verse five says, "who satisfies your desires with good things so that your youth is renewed like the eagle's." Our Heavenly Father knows what will satisfy us spiritually and physically and he gives us those things.

The Lord watches over the oppressed and will provide for them like he did for the Israelites when Moses led them out of Egypt. God is full of grace and mercy and he chooses to forgive our sins. "For as high as the heavens are above the earth, so great is his love for those who fear him; as far as the east is from the west, so far has he removed our transgressions from us (vv. 11-12). If we reverence and honor the Lord with our lives the love he has for us cannot be measured. He also puts our sins as far away from us as we can imagine.

Verses fifteen and sixteen say, "The life of mortals is like grass, they flourish like a flower of the field; the wind blows over it and it is gone, and its place remembers it no more." Our lives on this earth are numbered and temporary however God's love is eternal. His love is always with those who seek him.

There are many reasons to tell one's self to praise the Lord all day long. The question is are we doing it? We can give in to discouragement or we can choose to worship the Lord.

This Psalm ends with a call for all of God's creation in heaven and on the earth to praise the Lord. Let's join them and worship him today!

Reflection Questions

1. In light of this Psalm, when can talking to oneself be beneficial?
2. When do you find it difficult to praise the Lord?

Father, I choose to worship you today because of who you are and what you've done. I am so thankful for your love and that you forgive my sins. Let everything inside of me worship you today!

They Cried Out to the Lord

Give thanks to the LORD, for he is good; his love endures forever. Let the redeemed of the LORD tell their story—those he redeemed from the hand of the foe, those he gathered from the lands, from east and west, from north and south. Some wandered in desert wastelands, finding no way to a city where they could settle. They were hungry and thirsty, and their lives ebbed away. Then they cried out to the LORD in their trouble, and he delivered them from their distress. He led them by a straight way to a city where they could settle. Let them give thanks to the LORD for his unfailing love and his wonderful deeds for mankind, for he satisfies the thirsty and fills the hungry with good things. Some sat in darkness, in utter darkness, prisoners suffering in iron chains, because they rebelled against God's commands and despised the plans of the Most High. So he subjected them to bitter labor; they stumbled, and there was no one to help. Then they cried to the LORD in their trouble, and he saved them from their distress. He brought them out of darkness, the utter darkness, and broke away their chains. Let them give thanks to the LORD for his unfailing love and his wonderful deeds for mankind, for he breaks down gates of bronze and cuts through bars of iron. Some became fools through their rebellious ways and suffered affliction because of their iniquities. They loathed all food and drew near the gates of death. Then they cried to the LORD in their trouble, and he saved them from their distress.

PSALM 107:1-19

What do you do when you are in trouble? Sometimes our own decisions and sins bring trouble into our lives. Other times we are under attack by people.

There are many different scenarios given in this Psalm and each time it says, "Then they cried out to the Lord in their trouble". When they called on the Lord things changed in their lives. This is a Psalm of gratitude for God's goodness and love shown to his people.

In the first scenario they were wandering, hungry, and thirsty. "Then they cried out to the LORD in their trouble, and he delivered them from their distress" (v. 6). Our God hears and answers us when we call on him. Verse nine says, "...for he satisfies the thirsty and fills the hungry with good things". We forget that the Lord knows what we need better than we do. He knows which job we should have, the relationships we should invest in, and ultimately that only he can fill us spiritually.

In the second scenario God's people rebelled against him and ended up in prison and "So he subjected them to bitter labor" (v. 12). When they cried out to God he set them free from their chains. Jesus sets people free today from the power and bondage of sin. John 8:36 says, "So if the Son sets you free, you will be free indeed."

In the final scenario the people were close to death because of their sinful choices. God saved them when they called on his name. Are we quick to call on the Lord when we are in trouble or do we allow fear or pride to keep us from asking for help? When they called on the Lord he delivered them. We need to do the same.

Reflection Questions
1. What do you do when you are in trouble?
2. When have you "cried out to the Lord" for help?

Jesus, help me in the areas of trouble I am dealing with now. I pray that you would set me free from the power of sin and from any attacks of the evil one. Just as your people cried out to you I cry out to you believing that you will deliver me. (And Lord, might you receive the glory.)

WEEK

6

DAY 1 Disc 2 / Track 11

Ponder His Works

Praise the LORD. I will extol the LORD with all my heart in the council of the upright and in the assembly. Great are the works of the LORD; they are pondered by all who delight in them. Glorious and majestic are his deeds, and his righteousness endures forever. He has caused his wonders to be remembered; the Lord is gracious and compassionate. He provides food for those who fear him; he remembers his covenant forever. He has shown his people the power of his works, giving them the lands of other nations. The works of his hands are faithful and just; all his precepts are trustworthy. They are established for ever and ever, enacted in faithfulness and uprightness. He provided redemption for his people; he ordained his covenant forever—holy and awesome is his name. The fear of the LORD is the beginning of wisdom; all who follow his precepts have good understanding. To him belongs eternal praise.

PSALM 111:1-10

How much time do we spend thinking about God's deeds? We probably don't do it enough. This Psalm exhorts us to set our minds on what the Lord has done. I would venture to say many of us spend more time thinking about our problems and our needs rather than on God's amazing works.

After beginning with a call to exalt the Lord verse two says, "Great are the works of the LORD; they are pondered by all who delight in them." If we take joy in God's deeds then we will spend time thinking about them. Why is this so important? I think it builds our faith.

Verse four says, "...the LORD is gracious and compassionate." We need to be reminded of that when we are in need. However, it also helps us to remember to extend grace and compassion to others.

The Lord's provision, power, justice, faithfulness, and redemption are also mentioned in this Psalm. God has shown these qualities to his children and he continues to do so. Why should we fear when the all-powerful God of faithfulness and justice is our provider?

The Psalmist ends by saying, "The fear of the Lord is the beginning of wisdom; all who follow his precepts have good understanding. To him belongs eternal praise" (v. 10). Having awe and reverence for the Lord makes us wise. One of the ways we develop this healthy fear of the Lord is by thinking about the amazing things he has done for us personally and the things recorded in the Bible.

What are you thinking about today? If we think about God's works then we will join the Psalmist in praising the Lord!

Reflection Questions
1. What are some benefits of thinking about the Lord's deeds?
2. Verse 10 says, "The fear of the LORD is the beginning of wisdom". How can this healthy fear be developed in your life?

Father, I choose to think about your amazing works today. You have been faithful to your people throughout all generations in the Bible and I am thankful for your faithfulness to me as well.

DAY 2 Disc 2 / Track 12

Blessings for Those who Fear the Lord

*Blessed are those who fear the LORD, who find great delight in his com-
mands. Their children will be mighty in the land; the generation of the
upright will be blessed. Wealth and riches are in their houses, and their
righteousness endures forever. Even in darkness light dawns for the upright, for those who are gracious and compassionate and righteous. Good
will come to those who are generous and lend freely, who conduct their
affairs with justice. Surely the righteous will never be shaken; they will
be remembered forever. They will have no fear of bad news; their hearts
are steadfast, trusting in the LORD. Their hearts are secure, they will
have no fear; in the end they will look in triumph on their foes.*

PSALM 112:1-8

This Psalm lists blessings for those who fear the Lord and delight in
his law. "Their children will be mighty in the land" (v. 2). When we
follow after God and find our joy in obeying him there is a blessing
that is passed down to our children. They learn to put the Lord first
in their lives too.

"Wealth and riches are in their houses, and their righteousness
endures forever" (v. 3). Those who follow after God have spiritual
and material blessings. Their righteousness will last. We know that
since Christ died for our sins that our righteousness is truly only
found in him.

"Even in darkness light dawns for the upright, for those who
are gracious and compassionate and righteous" (v. 4). Even in our
toughest times, the Lord shines his light on the way of those who
seek him. Those who fear him are firmly established. They leave a
legacy of following the Lord for their children, grandchildren, and

the others who know them. That is how they're remembered.

Verses six and seven tell us that when we follow the Lord we don't fear bad news because our hearts are constant in seeking God. We don't have to be afraid because our trust is not in our health, job, and other physical things. It is in the Lord and his promises.

Lastly, those who fear the Lord triumph over their enemies, but the way of the wicked will come to nothing.

Reflection Questions

1. How do you want to be remembered?
2. What kind of spiritual legacy are you leaving for your children or for others over whom you have influence?

Lord I want to leave a legacy of loving and serving you, and blessing for my children and for those over whom you've given me influence. Help me to be constant in seeking you so I will not fear difficult things but will trust in you.

DAY 3 Disc 2 / Track 13

Why So Much Suffering?

Because he turned his ear to me, I will call on him as long as I live. The cords of death entangled me, the anguish of the grave came over me; I was overcome by distress and sorrow. Then I called on the name of the LORD: "LORD, save me!" The LORD is gracious and righteous; our God is full of compassion. The LORD protects the unwary; when I was brought low, he saved me. Return to your rest, my soul, for the LORD has been good to you. For you, LORD, have delivered me from death, my eyes from tears, my feet from stumbling, that I may walk before the LORD in the land of the living. I trusted in the LORD when I said, "I am greatly afflicted"; in my alarm I said, "Everyone is a liar." What shall I return to the LORD for all his goodness to me? I will lift up the cup of salvation and call on the name of the LORD. I will fulfill my vows to the LORD in the presence of all his people. Precious in the sight of the LORD is the death of his faithful servants. Truly I am your servant, LORD; I serve you just as my mother did; you have freed me from my chains. I will sacrifice a thank offering to you and call on the name of the LORD. I will fulfill my vows to the LORD in the presence of all his people, in the courts of the house of the LORD—in your midst, Jerusalem.

PSALM 116:2-19

Why does the Lord allow so much suffering in our lives? I don't have the answer for that. Nothing is ever perfect in this life as we are always in a trial or one is on the way.

This Psalm like many of the others is written from a place of hardship. The writer was near death and full of trouble and sorrow. Then he cried out to the Lord for help and he was delivered. God showed mercy, grace, and compassion.

Why are so many of the Psalms written from a place of great distress and trouble? Why is this the norm?

Here is a quote from Randy Alcorn's book *If God is Good*, "Joni

Eareckson Tada writes, 'God permits what he hates to accomplish that which he loves.'[20] Evil is never good, yet God can use any evil to accomplish good and sovereign purposes. Through the redemptive suffering of Christ—in which he took all human evils on himself—and through his triumph over evil and death, God has done everything necessary to defeat evil."[21]

The Lord had his son Jesus suffer and die a painful death on the cross so that we could be forgiven of our sins. Our salvation and eternal joy and happiness hinges on a tragic event that was filled with pain and suffering. Why wouldn't we also suffer in this life?

1 Peter 4:12-13 says, "Dear friends, do not be surprised at the fiery ordeal that has come on you to test you, as though something strange were happening to you. But rejoice insomuch as you participate in the sufferings of Christ, so that you may be overjoyed when his glory is revealed."

Rather than being surprised when we suffer we are told to rejoice that we are able to join Christ in his sufferings now knowing that our joy will be full when we are in his presence forever.

The Psalmist asks how he can repay the Lord for helping him in his time of need. He calls on God's name, fulfills his vows, declares himself a servant of the Lord, and brings sacrifices of thanksgiving. The proper response for God's deliverance and help is to first express our gratitude and praise to him for it. Then we should fully devote ourselves to following after him and his ways.[22]

However we are reminded in the Psalms that more troubles will come. Our devotion to the Lord is ultimately founded on who he is and not just his willingness and ability to save us in times of need.

Reflection Questions

1. Why do you think God allows suffering in our lives?
2. How can Jesus' death on the cross change our perspective on our own suffering?

Father, give me your view on the sufferings you allow in my life. I want my sufferings to give you glory and to draw me closer to you.

DAY 4 ● Disc 2 / Track 14

Your Word is Perfect

Your word, LORD, is eternal; it stands firm in the heavens. Your faithfulness continues through all generations; you established the earth, and it endures. Your laws endure to this day, for all things serve you. If your law had not been my delight, I would have perished in my affliction. I will never forget your precepts, for by them you have preserved my life. Save me, for I am yours; I have sought out your precepts. The wicked are waiting to destroy me, but I will ponder your statutes. To all perfection I see a limit, but your commands are boundless. Oh, how I love your law! I meditate on it all day long. Your commands are always with me and make me wiser than my enemies. I have more insight than all my teachers, for I meditate on your statutes. I have more understanding than the elders, for I obey your precepts. I have kept my feet from every evil path so that I might obey your word. I have not departed from your laws, for you yourself have taught me. How sweet are your words to my taste, sweeter than honey to my mouth! I gain understanding from your precepts; therefore I hate every wrong path.

PSALM 119:89-104

This short section taken from the longest Psalm boasts about the greatness of God's Word. His Word and his faithfulness will last forever. This Psalm emphasizes again the importance of delighting in God's Word. "If your law had not been my delight, I would have perished in my affliction" (v. 92). When we are in challenging times it is the promises and hope from scripture that keep us going. We can delight in God's Word at all times-especially when storms surround us. In those times our delight is based on his truth and not on joyful emotions because they aren't always there.

The Psalmist acknowledges that God's Word is perfect and isn't limited in its perfection like other things. Verses ninety-seven through one hundred say, "Oh, how I love your law! I meditate on it all day long. Your commands are always with me and make me wiser than my enemies. I have more insight than all my teachers, for I meditate on your statutes. I have more understanding than the elders, for I obey your precepts." If we love God's law we will meditate on it and find our joy in it.

Do we think about the promises of scripture throughout our days? His Word makes us wiser than those around us but most importantly it can keep us in a close relationship to the Lord. If we value the Lord and his Word above all else than it will keep our feet from sinful paths. We will long to read it, meditate on it, and follow it.

There are many good books that I have enjoyed reading over the years but there is no book like the Bible. It provides hope, encouragement, and direction like no other book. Like this Psalm says, it is truly perfect!

Reflection Questions

1. How should the knowledge that God's Word is perfect affect us?
2. Do you love and delight in God's Word? How can you grow in this area?

Lord, your Word is perfect. Help me to value your Word above every other book. I choose to delight in your Word knowing that it provides the best roadmap for life.

DAY 5   Disc 2 / Track 15

The Lord Watches over You

I lift up my eyes to the mountains—where does my help come from? My help comes from the LORD, the Maker of heaven and earth. He will not let your foot slip—he who watches over you will not slumber; indeed, he who watches over Israel will neither slumber nor sleep. The LORD watches over you—the LORD is your shade at your right hand; the sun will not harm you by day, nor the moon by night. The LORD will keep you from all harm—he will watch over your life; the LORD will watch over your coming and going both now and forevermore.

PSALM 121:1-8

This Psalm begins by asking where our help comes from. Our help comes from our creator God. "He will not let your foot slip-he who watches over you will not slumber; indeed, he who watches over Israel will neither slumber nor sleep" (vv. 3-4).

When hiking I have helped others when they slip and I have been steadied by others when I have lost my footing. In life there are many things that come against us that can cause us to fall but the Lord keeps our feet secure. God will never be caught sleeping on the job. His watchful eyes are always watching over his children.

Like a loving father keeps a protective eye on his children the Lord watches out for us. Our human ability to protect others falls short but God's protective power is limitless.

In the same way we take shade from the sun the Lord shades us from things that can harm us. For example, some people can cause us great harm or distress in life. Although relationships can be affirming and life giving they can also be detrimental. The Lord watches over us and protects us even when others are out to cause damage in our lives.

Finally this Psalm ends with a promise that the Lord will watch over us forever. Are we looking to the Lord to protect us or do we put our trust in our cars, money, and other things? As Psalm 20:7 says, "Some trust in chariots and some in horses, but we trust in the Name of the Lord our God."

Reflection Questions

1. Have you ever been saved from falling by someone steadying you or catching you? What happened?
2. Verse 3 says, "He will not let your foot slip-- he who watches over you will not slumber". How does this verse encourage you today?

Lord thank you for watching over me at all times. I choose to look to you as the source of my protection and help rather than looking to other things. I ask you to watch over my family and those I love. Thank you for keeping my feet secure when my footing gets loose.

DAY 6  Disc 2 / Track 16

Unless the Lord Builds the House

Unless the LORD builds the house, the builders labor in vain. Unless the LORD watches over the city, the guards stand watch in vain. In vain you rise early and stay up late, toiling for food to eat—for he grants sleep to those he loves. Children are a heritage from the LORD, offspring a reward from him. Like arrows in the hands of a warrior are children born in one's youth. Blessed is the man whose quiver is full of them. They will not be put to shame when they contend with their opponents in court.

PSALM 127:1-5

Do we approach each day asking God to lead and guide us? This Psalm reminds us that God is sovereign over all things. We can make our plans and pursue them but "Unless the LORD builds the house, the builders labor in vain" (v. 1). The Lord has the final word on the outcome of our work and our family.

God is also the ultimate protector. Human security only goes so far. "Unless the LORD watches over the city, the guards stand watch in vain" (v. 1). At times we try to follow God in our own strength and yet the outcome can be disastrous. We can become workaholics all for the sake of what we call "serving God". However this Psalm reminds us that, "...he grants sleep to those he loves" (v. 2). Our Father doesn't want us to be stressed out by burning the candle at both ends. He wants to give us the rest we need as we follow him.

The Psalmist says that children are a reward from the Lord. They are compared to arrows as a source of defense or protection for their parents.[23]

My wife Gretchen and I are blessed to have three boys: Nathan

(2004), Nicholas (2006), and Noah (2010). I am amazed at how quickly they can come to our defense if they think we are being wronged. We are thankful for them and know that each of them is truly a blessing from the Lord as this Psalm says.

In each of our families let's remember that God is the builder of our house and allow him to lead the way.

Reflection Questions
1. How are children a reward from the Lord?
2. How does knowing God has the final say on the outcomes in your life affect you?

Father, I pray that you would lead my family as we seek to follow you. I pray that you would lead me in all of my endeavors today. Help me to find my rest in you and to depend on you in all things.

DAY 7   Disc 2 / Track 17

Walk in His Ways

Blessed are all who fear the LORD, who walk in obedience to him. You will eat the fruit of your labor; blessings and prosperity will be yours. Your wife will be like a fruitful vine within your house; your children will be like olive shoots around your table. Yes, this will be the blessing for the man who fears the LORD. May the LORD bless you from Zion; may you see the prosperity of Jerusalem all the days of your life. May you live to see your children's children—peace be on Israel.

PSALM 128:1-6

The most important human relationships we have are our families. Is this true of us in a practical way? Do our families come before all the other relationships in our lives?

As a pastor I sometimes feel the tension between loving my family and loving my church. I am called to love and care for both of them; however, my first calling is to my family. In reality my effectiveness as a minister is greatly reduced if I don't love my family well. The same is true for all of us. We need to make our families the priority they should be.

This Psalm like the last one focuses on the family. There is a blessing for those who walk according to God's ways. Their work will be fruitful and they will be prosperous. Their families will also be blessed. When we give our families the attention and support they need it gives them a solid foundation from which to grow. We show them the love of God in tangible ways. 1 John 4:11 says, "Dear friends, since God so loved us, we also ought to love one another."

Part of the blessing is being able to live to see grandchildren grow up. It is a joy for my wife Gretchen and I to watch our parents experience the joys of knowing their grandkids. They have the privilege of loving them, encouraging them, befriending them, and being a listening ear. Most importantly they have the privilege of being a part of passing onto them the legacy of a godly heritage. This Psalm underscores the importance of that.

Reflection Questions

1. Did a grandparent make a positive difference in your life? What did they do?
2. Does your family know they are more important to you than your job? If so, how do they know?

Lord, I am thankful that you created and value the family unit. Thank you for the family that you have given me. I desire to love them in a way that honors you. Help me to "walk in your ways" when it comes to my family.

WEEK

7

DAY 1

Wait for the Lord

Out of the depths I cry to you, LORD; Lord, hear my voice. Let your ears be attentive to my cry for mercy. If you, LORD, kept a record of sins, Lord, who could stand? But with you there is forgiveness, so that we can, with reverence, serve you. I wait for the LORD, my whole being waits, and in his word I put my hope. I wait for the LORD more than watchmen wait for the morning, more than watchmen wait for the morning. Israel, put your hope in the LORD, for with the LORD is unfailing love and with him is full redemption. He himself will redeem Israel from all their sins.

PSALM 130:1-8

Do you remember longing to open up Christmas presents as a kid? I remember guessing what my presents were and then wishing I could play with them right away.

This Psalm is one of confession and repentance and yet it also contains a longing and waiting on the Lord to move. The Psalmist begins by crying out to God in his pain, misery, and sin. He asks God to have mercy on him and then says, "If you, LORD, kept a record of sins, Lord, who could stand?" (v. 3).

I am so glad that God doesn't hold my sins against me. He puts them as far as the "east is from the west".[24] Romans 8:1 says "...there is now no condemnation for those who are in Christ Jesus". I don't have to feel bad about things for which God has forgiven me.

Then the Psalmist compares his waiting on God to those who stood guard waiting for the morning. He says his longing and waiting for God is stronger. What was he waiting for? I think he was waiting for deliverance, encouragement, restoration, and direction.

When we are in troubled times we need to ask God for help and encouragement. When we have sinned we need to ask God to restore us to a right relationship with him and give us direction in those areas of our lives.

Notice that he put his hope in God's Word while he was waiting. While we are waiting on God do we study, meditate on, and put our hope in his Word? His Word assures us that his love lasts forever and he is quick to forgive and lead us onward.

Reflection Questions

1. What do you have a hard time waiting for?
2. While waiting on God, how can you put your hope in his Word?

Lord I wait on you today. I ask for forgiveness for wrong thoughts, words, and actions. As I wait for your deliverance and help I put my hope in your Word. I am thankful that your love lasts forever. Thank you for your forgiveness.

DAY 2 Disc 2 / Track 19

Pleasant Unity

How good and pleasant it is when God's people live together in unity! It is like precious oil poured on the head, running down on the beard, running down on Aaron's beard, down on the collar of his robe. It is as if the dew of Hermon were falling on Mount Zion. For there the LORD bestows his blessing, even life forevermore.

PSALM 133:1-3

There is something amazing that happens when God's people live, fellowship, and work together in unity. During my time working with Youth With a Mission I helped organize worship and prayer nights that united Christians from many different denominations. When they came together in unity the groundwork was laid for many new people to become followers of Christ in their city.

As a pastor I have watched amazing things happen when people join together to raise funds, work on projects, etc. I have also seen disunity bring hardship and destruction to relationships and church life. It has been sad and painful to watch and experience.

This Psalm says it so well. "How good and pleasant it is when God's people live together in unity" (v. 1). It is not only good but it is an amazingly joyful and enjoyable experience!

Unity is compared to anointing oil that went on the head and ran down Aaron's beard. Anointing someone was a sign of God setting someone apart for himself. Unity sets people apart in a special way for God's service.

Unity is also compared to the dew of Hermon that brought physical blessing or fruitfulness on the land.[25] Unity among followers of Jesus brings fruitfulness too.

Jesus talks about unity in John 17:20-21, "My prayer is not for them alone. I pray also for those who will believe in me through their message, that all of them may be one, Father, just as you are in me and I am in you. May they also be in us so that the world may believe that you have sent me."

Jesus was praying that his followers would be unified like he was with his Father so that people would believe in him. We need to pray for that kind of unity in our relationships so that people would follow Jesus as a result. When Christians truly love each other and work together it is attractive. It makes people want to follow Jesus!

Reflection Questions

1. Have you seen God's people work together in incredible ways? What was the result?
2. What can you do to have greater unity in your relationships?

Lord, help me live in unity with the brothers and sisters you have put around me. I want to have biblical unity that is a witness to others of your greatness and power.

DAY 3   Disc 2 / Track 20

The Lord's Name and Fame Endure

Praise the LORD. Praise the name of the LORD; praise him, you servants of the LORD, you who minister in the house of the LORD, in the courts of the house of our God. Praise the LORD, for the LORD is good; sing praise to his name, for that is pleasant. For the LORD has chosen Jacob to be his own, Israel to be his treasured possession. I know that the LORD is great, that our Lord is greater than all gods. The LORD does whatever pleases him, in the heavens and on the earth, in the seas and all their depths. He makes clouds rise from the ends of the earth; he sends lightning with the rain and brings out the wind from his storehouses. He struck down the firstborn of Egypt, the firstborn of people and animals. He sent his signs and wonders into your midst, Egypt, against Pharaoh and all his servants. He struck down many nations and killed mighty kings—Sihon king of the Amorites, Og king of Bashan, and all the kings of Canaan—and he gave their land as an inheritance, an inheritance to his people Israel. Your name, LORD, endures forever, your renown, LORD, through all generations.

PSALM 135:1-13

This song of praise begins with a call to those "...who minister in the house of the Lord" (v. 2). The priests ministered in God's house in the Old Testament.

As a pastor I consider it a privilege to work in the house of the Lord where praising him is of utmost importance. Worshipping the Lord isn't simply my job; it is a lifestyle and a privilege.

"Praise the LORD, for the LORD is good; sing praise to his name, for that is pleasant" (v. 3). We worship the Lord for his goodness. Praising the Lord is a joyful experience. Pleasant people have a way of making us feel special and they can transform routine things into interesting experiences. I look forward to being around people like that. In a much greater way being in the presence of the Lord is an incredibly pleasant and uplifting experience.

This Psalm tells us that the Lord is great, he does what he pleases, and all creation obeys him. He performed many miracles in Egypt and had his people Israel conquer many nations and kings.

Verse thirteen says, "Your name, LORD, endures forever, your renown, LORD, through all generations." The Lord's name and fame will last forever. Famous people come and go in this world. Professional athletes can only stay at the top of their game for a few years, politician's terms come to an end, a great singer's voice deteriorates over time, and someone more talented always comes along.

The Bible tells of the greatness of the Lord and of his amazing exploits. He is omniscient (all-knowing), omnipotent (all-powerful), omnipresent (everywhere at the same time), and will rule heaven and the new earth forever. We will get the privilege of being in his presence and worshipping him forever!

Reflection Questions

1. Is praising the Lord a pleasant experience for you? Why or why not?
2. Verse 13 says, "Your name, O LORD, endures forever, your renown, O LORD, through all generations." How can this verse give you hope today?

Jesus, I look forward to being fully in your presence. I'm thankful that your name and your fame will endure forever. I consider it my privilege, pleasure, and joy to worship you and live for you today.

DAY 4 Disc 2 / Track 21

Your Name and Word Exalted

I give you thanks, O LORD, with my whole heart; before the gods I sing your praise; I bow down toward your holy temple and give thanks to your name for your steadfast love and your faithfulness, for you have exalted above all things your name and your word. On the day I called, you answered me; my strength of soul you increased. All the kings of the earth shall give you thanks, O LORD, for they have heard the words of your mouth, and they shall sing of the ways of the LORD, for great is the glory of the LORD. For though the LORD is high, he regards the lowly, but the haughty he knows from afar. Though I walk in the midst of trouble, you preserve my life; you stretch out your hand against the wrath of my enemies, and your right hand delivers me. The LORD will fulfill his purpose for me; your steadfast love, O LORD, endures forever. Do not forsake the work of your hands.

PSALM 138:1-8 (ESV)

I'm thankful that the Lord has exalted his name and his Word above all things. There is security in knowing that God and his Word stand prominently above all else he has created in heaven and on the earth.

Colossians 1:17 says, "He is before all things, and in him all things hold together." Jesus' name is above all things and he keeps everything working together.

The psalmist begins by expressing his desire to worship God with his whole heart and he worships him for his love and faithfulness. How often do we thank God for his "love (that) has been poured out into our hearts"[26] and for his constant faithfulness in our lives? When we think of the ways God has shown us his love and faithfulness we can't help but be filled with gratitude and praise to

Jesus.

The psalmist mentions God's help in trouble and the need for the kings of the earth to worship the Lord. "...and they shall sing of the ways of the Lord, for great is the glory of the Lord. For though the Lord is high, he regards the lowly," (vv. 5-6-ESV). Even though God is great and mighty, he values and responds positively to humility in our lives. He will help us in troubled times and his purposes will ultimately be accomplished in our lives.

I sometimes question whether the things going on in my life and in the lives of those close to me will turn out for good. However I often look at things from a selfish perspective but this Psalm reminds me that God's purposes and ways are bigger than me.

Reflection Questions

1. How often do you thank the Lord for his love and faithfulness? What helps you remember to do that?
2. How does knowing God's purposes will be accomplished in your life change your outlook on your present circumstances?

Lord I am thankful that you have lifted your name and your Word above all things. I take comfort in the fact that you are working out your purposes in my life today.

DAY 5   Disc 2 / Track 22

The Lord Knows Us

You have searched me, Lord, and you know me. You know when I sit and when I rise; you perceive my thoughts from afar. You discern my going out and my lying down; you are familiar with all my ways. Before a word is on my tongue you, Lord, know it completely. You hem me in behind and before, and you lay your hand upon me. Such knowledge is too wonderful for me, too lofty for me to attain. Where can I go from your Spirit? Where can I flee from your presence? If I go up to the heavens, you are there; if I make my bed in the depths, you are there. If I rise on the wings of the dawn, if I settle on the far side of the sea, even there your hand will guide me, your right hand will hold me fast. If I say, "Surely the darkness will hide me and the light become night around me," even the darkness will not be dark to you; the night will shine like the day, for darkness is as light to you. For you created my inmost being; you knit me together in my mother's womb. I praise you because I am fearfully and wonderfully made; your works are wonderful, I know that full well. My frame was not hidden from you when I was made in the secret place, when I was woven together in the depths of the earth. Your eyes saw my unformed body; all the days ordained for me were written in your book before one of them came to be. How precious to me are your thoughts, God! How vast is the sum of them! Were I to count them, they would outnumber the grains of sand—when I awake, I am still with you. Search me, God, and know my heart; test me and know my anxious thoughts. See if there is any offensive way in me, and lead me in the way everlasting.

PSALM 139:1-18, 23-24

Do you ever wonder if God really knows you? This Psalm lets us know that God created us, knows everything about us, and we cannot hide from his presence. This is great news for the person who loves the Lord and wants to please him with their lives.

God knows our thoughts, our words, and our actions. His protective eye is watching over us. "You hem me in behind and before, and you lay your hand upon me. Such knowledge is too wonderful for me" (vv. 5-6).

David rejoiced in this news and so should we. The Bible makes it clear that God has good plans for us and wants the best for us. Knowing that he is always with us and is watching over us should bring peace, comfort, and security to us.

Verse twelve says, "even the darkness will not be dark to you; the night will shine like the day, for darkness is as light to you." God is able to shine his light into our lives in our darkest moments. I am so thankful that he is always with us.

If we ever question the unchangeable things in our lives like the family we were born into or the physical makeup we were given we need to remember this: "For you created my inmost being; you knit me together in my mother's womb. I praise you because I am fearfully and wonderfully made" (vv. 13-14). The Lord created and formed us with great care and love. We may not like everything he has given us but we can choose to glorify him with our lives. He knows what is going to happen before it happens so we can trust his plans for us. His thoughts toward us are good.

David ends the Psalm by asking God to search him, test him, and know his anxieties. He is also asking God to root out any sin in his life. Knowing that the Lord knows everything about us and he knows what is going to happen to us can help us to yield our anxieties and worries to him today.

Reflection Questions

1. Do you believe you are "fearfully and wonderfully made" by God? (v. 14) If so, how does that affect the way you see yourself?

2. In light of this Psalm, how should you view the unchangeable things in your life?

Father, I take comfort in knowing that you formed me in my mother's womb and you know me completely. I yield my anxieties to you today asking you to lead me in your paths.

DAY 6  Disc 2 / Track 23

Keep Me From Evildoers

I call to you, LORD, come quickly to me; hear me when I call to you. May my prayer be set before you like incense; may the lifting up of my hands be like the evening sacrifice. Set a guard over my mouth, LORD; keep watch over the door of my lips. Do not let my heart be drawn to what is evil so that I take part in wicked deeds along with those who are evildoers; do not let me eat their delicacies. Let a righteous man strike me— that is a kindness; let him rebuke me—that is oil on my head. My head will not refuse it, for my prayer will still be against the deeds of evildoers. Their rulers will be thrown down from the cliffs, and the wicked will learn that my words were well spoken. They will say, "As one plows and breaks up the earth, so our bones have been scattered at the mouth of the grave." But my eyes are fixed on you, Sovereign LORD; in you I take refuge—do not give me over to death. Keep me safe from the traps set by evildoers, from the snares they have laid for me. Let the wicked fall into their own nets, while I pass by in safety.

PSALM 141:1-10

This Psalm is a cry to God asking for help to stay away from the ways of evildoers. David asks for the Lord's help and to hear his prayer.

Then he says, "Set a guard over my mouth, LORD; keep watch over the door of my lips. Do not let my heart be drawn to what is evil, so that I take part in wicked deeds along with those who are evildoers; do not let me eat their delicacies" (vv. 3-4). How often do our mouths get us in trouble when we say things that we shouldn't? The book of James calls the tongue a "fire".[27] We need to guard the things we say knowing what comes out of our mouth is a sign of what is inside of us.

David compares the ways of evildoers to fine foods. Sin is attractive but it always bites back with unwanted consequences and most importantly it hurts our relationship with the Lord.

Then he talks about the blessing when a righteous person speaks the truth to us in love. Proverbs 27:6 says, "Wounds from a friend can be trusted, but an enemy multiplies kisses." We don't like to be rebuked or corrected but it can be a true blessing when it comes from those who love us.

I am thankful for the many people who have spoken into my life at different times. I remember telling someone once that I would never want to do a certain type of job. They told me that I needed to be willing to do what God wanted me to. About five years later I was asked to do that type of a job. I think that person's words may have been the Lord preparing me for what was coming.

Verse eight of the Psalm says, "But my eyes are fixed on you, Sovereign LORD; in you I take refuge-do not give me over to death." In contrast to the ways of the wicked David says that his eyes are on the Lord. His focus is on pleasing the Lord and not on following evildoers. He ends by asking God to protect him in all his ways.

Reflection Questions

1. Can you think of a time when your mouth got you in trouble? What happened?

2. Do you have good friends around you who will speak the truth to you even when it hurts? If not, how can you develop those relationships?

Lord, I look to you today. I want to follow in your ways and not the ways of evildoers. I choose to listen to the wise counselors you put around me that help me hear your voice.

DAY 7 Disc 2 / Track 24

The Lord Delights in Us

Praise the LORD. How good it is to sing praises to our God, how pleasant and fitting to praise him! The LORD builds up Jerusalem; he gathers the exiles of Israel. He heals the brokenhearted and binds up their wounds. He determines the number of the stars and calls them each by name. Great is our Lord and mighty in power; his understanding has no limit. The LORD sustains the humble but casts the wicked to the ground. Sing to the LORD with grateful praise; make music to our God on the harp. He covers the sky with clouds; he supplies the earth with rain and makes grass grow on the hills. He provides food for the cattle and for the young ravens when they call. His pleasure is not in the strength of the horse, nor his delight in the legs of the warrior; the LORD delights in those who fear him, who put their hope in his unfailing love.

PSALM 147:1-11

As we have been reading these Psalms, we have been seeking to delight in the Lord on a daily basis by delighting in his law.

This Psalm tells us that, "...the Lord delights in those who fear him" (v. 11). Zephaniah 3:17 says, "He will take great delight in you; in his love he will no longer rebuke you, but will rejoice over you with singing." The Lord takes joy in us and rejoices over us when we seek after him.

In the same way a parent sings to their child at night when he is troubled, God sings over us. I cannot imagine how amazing it would sound to hear the creator of music sing! I hope to get that experience in heaven.

We sometimes look for our joy in the things of this earth and in people but those things don't impress the Lord. He delights in those whose hearts are turned towards him. That is another reason to praise the Lord. Verse one says, "Praise the LORD. How good it is to sing praises to our God, how pleasant and fitting to praise him!"

This Psalm describes God as healer, creator, and sustainer. He heals the hurting, has created the universe, and sustains both his people and his creation.

Verse five says that God's "...understanding has no limit". King Solomon was the wisest man who ever lived but his wisdom had limitations. God's wisdom has no borders and that is the reason that we need to be constantly seeking his help in prayer. He will guide and direct us in our decisions.

James 1:5 says, "If any of you lacks wisdom, you should ask God, who gives generously to all without finding fault, and it will be given to you." Wisdom is one gift the Bible specifically tells us to ask for so this gift must be important. Let's ask for his wisdom today knowing that he delights in those who seek him!

Reflection Questions

1. How does it make you feel to know that the Lord delights in you when you seek him?

2. When was the last time you asked God for wisdom? In what area do you need wisdom today?

Lord I ask for wisdom today. Thank you for the promise that you delight in me and rejoice over me with singing. I worship you today as I delight in you and your greatness!

BONUS   Disc 2 / Track 25

Let Everything Praise the Lord

*Praise the LORD. Praise God in his sanctuary; praise him in his mighty
heavens. Praise him for his acts of power; praise him for his surpassing
greatness. Praise him with the sounding of the trumpet, praise him with
the harp and lyre, praise him with timbrel and dancing, praise him with
the strings and pipe, praise him with the clash of cymbals, praise him
with resounding cymbals. Let everything that has breath praise the
LORD. Praise the LORD.*

PSALM 150:1-6

This simple Psalm begins by telling us where God should be praised.
He is to be praised "...in his sanctuary" (v. 1) and in the heavens.

Then we are told why to praise him. We praise him for his acts of
power and his greatness. Scripture tells us story after story showing
his power and supreme greatness. A few examples are: The creation
of the heavens and the earth, the parting of the Red Sea, Daniel being saved in the Lion's Den, the miracles of Jesus, and many more.

Then we are told to praise him with musical instruments and
dancing. David mentions the trumpet, harp, lyre, timbrel, strings,
pipe, and cymbals. I would add guitars, keyboards, and every other
orchestral instrument not mentioned.

Finally we are told who should praise the Lord. "Let everything
that has breath praise the Lord" (v. 6). This Psalm says that the Lord
is to be worshipped everywhere, with every musical instrument,
and by everyone with breath.

As we have examined how to delight in the Lord through the
Psalms some themes have emerged. The writers of the Psalms were
often in trouble or in difficult situations. Themes of God's deliver-

ance, safety, and protection are frequent. Themes of trusting, loving, and finding our strength in the Lord are prominent as well. The overarching theme is the greatness, power, majesty, and glory of the Lord.

When we are seeking to delight in the Lord at all times remembering his greatness and power helps us get our focus off of our troubles and the things of this world so we can put our attention fully on him!

Reflection Questions

1. This Psalm says that the Lord is to be praised everywhere, with every instrument, by everyone. How and where do you praise the Lord?

2. In what ways have you learned to delight in the Lord while reading this devotional? How does focusing on God's glory and greatness change your outlook on life?

Father, I choose to praise you everywhere, at all times, and in every way I can. Thank you for teaching me to delight in you and your Word through the Psalms. I choose to focus on your glory and goodness today!

1. Merriam-Webster online dictionary, http://www.merriam-webster.com/dictionary/meditate.

2. The Arrow Leadership program trains Christian leaders in North America and beyond to be "led more by Jesus, lead more like Jesus and lead more to Jesus." www.arrowleadership.org.

3. Louie Giglio, *The Air I Breathe* (Sisters, Ore.: Multnomah, 2003), 31.

4. John Piper, *Desiring God* (Colorado Springs, Co.: Multnomah, 1986, 1996, 2003, 2011), these thoughts from or influenced by this book.

5. John Piper, *Desiring God*, 10.

6. John Piper, *Future Grace* (Colorado Springs, Co.: Multnomah, 1995, 2012), introduction 1, chapter 3, chapter 24.

7. Randy Alcorn, *Heaven* (Carol Stream, Ill.: Tyndale, 2004), 191.

8. Kenneth L. Barker, *New International Version Study Bible*, (Grand Rapids, Mi.: Zondervan, 1985, 1995, 2002), 1075-1076.

9. Matthew Henry, *Psalms. Matthew Henry Commentary on the Whole Bible (Complete)*. N.p. (1706), http://www.biblestudytools.com/commentaries/matthew-henry-complete/psalms-1-75/

10. Matthew Henry, *Psalms. Matthew Henry Commentary on the Whole Bible (Complete)*.

11. Samuel 21:12-13.

12. Jamieson-Fausset-Brown, *Psalms. Jamieson-Fausset-Brown Bible Commentary (Complete)*. N.p. (1871) http://www.biblestudytools.com/commentaries/jamieson-fausset-brown/psalms-1-75/.

13. Acts 13:22.

14. Jamieson-Fausset-Brown, *Psalms. Jamieson-Fausset-Brown Bible Commentary (Complete).*

15. Jamieson-Fausset-Brown, *Psalms.* Jamieson-Fausset-Brown Bible Commentary (Complete).

16. John Piper, *Desiring God.*

17. Kenneth L. Barker, *New International Version Study Bible*, 1178-1179.

18. Kenneth L. Barker, *New International Version Study Bible*, 1178.

19. Kenneth L. Barker, *New International Version Study Bible*, 1197.

20. Joni Eareckson Tada, *Pearls of Great Price: 366 Daily Devotional Readings* (Grand Rapids, Mi: Zondervan, 2006), 387.

21. Randy Alcorn. *If God Is Good* (Colorado Springs, Co.: Multnomah, 2009), 34.

22. Kenneth L. Barker, *New International Version Study Bible*, 1231.

23. Jamieson-Fausset-Brown, *Psalms. Jamieson-Fausset-Brown Bible Commentary (Complete).* N.p. (1871), http://www.biblestudytools.com/commentaries/jamieson-fausset-brown/psalms-76-150/.

24. Psalm 103:12.

25. Jamieson-Fausset-Brown, *Psalms. Jamieson-Fausset-Brown Bible Commentary (Complete).*

26. Romans 5:5.

27. James 3:6.